21.95

The Inner Circle

Seven Gates to Marriage

The Inner Circle

 FELDHEIM PUBLISHERS Jerusalem/New York

Seven Gates to Marriage

by Shaya Ostrov, CSW

To contact Shaya Ostrov
please call **(718) 337-0824,**
or log onto our website at
www.7gates.com

First published, 2000

ISBN 1-58330-397-9

© Copyright 2000 by Shaya Ostrov

All rights reserved

No part of this publication may be translated, reproduced, stored in a retrieval system or transmitted, in any form or by any means, electronic, mechanical, photocopying, recording or otherwise, without prior permission in writing from the publishers.

FELDHEIM PUBLISHERS
200 Airport Executive Park
Nanuet NY 10954

POB 35002 / Jerusalem, Israel

www.feldheim.com

Printed in Israel

*This work is dedicated
to the memory of my late father*

יצחק יונה בן מאיר ע"ה

*who, since his passing in 1954,
has been at the heart
of my inner circle.
The doros of an unbroken chain
of true baalei chesed and bnei Torah,
from the Kaufman, Schreiber
and Ostrov families, give ongoing testimony
to the greatness of his legacy.*

ביהמ"ד גבול יעבץ
ברוקלין, נוא יארק

דוד קאהן

ב"ה

The Talmud (Kesuvos 67b) teaches us that within the commandment to help the poor is included helping someone to get married. The verse (Devarim 15:8) "You shall open your hand to him, lend him that which he requires, whatever he lacks, that is lacking to him", is disected. "Whatever he lacks" refers to a dwelling place; "that is lacking" refers to bed and table; "to him" refers to a mate. It is noteworthy that home, bed and table are not particularly subjective. Any kind will do. A mate is, however, something which is "to him".

Due to sociological changes that our era has been subjected to it has been difficult for us to cope with the manifold problems we have been confronted with. Our commitment to Torah values makes our alignment with our epoch both trying and challenging.

One of the great upheavals from yesterday's norm is the manner of finding a mate. Not so very long ago, the parents were the prime movers with but nodding acquiescence of the principals. Today, the burden of decision is on the shoulders of the men and women seeking a mate. The realization that this decision concerning one's life is so paramount, stifles many people from coming to a conclusion.

There are many individuals who are dedicated to help singles find their mates. The task is Herculean since there is no trodden path to follow.

Reb Shaya Ostrov has made a significant contribution towards solving this problem by detailing a program to focus on the prime objective for dating. A more apt description would be that this work instructs the dates to concentrate on the purpose of every meeting so that it should serve as a cohesive step towards the voyage that leads to matrimony.

Mr. Ostrov has tempered his academic knowledge with psychological insight and pragmatic experience to create this book. I say "More Power" to him. May he be fortunate that this serves as a model to fulfill the above mentioned imperative.

דוד קאהן
סיון תשנ"ז

Letter of approbation from Rabbi Dovid Cohen, Shlita

Rav Yaakov Reisman   בס״ד   יעקב רייזמאנן
104 Cumberland Place   רב דק״ק אגודת ישראל
Lawrence, N.Y. 11559   סניף לאנג איילאנד

24 Sivan, 5759
June 8, 1999

We are experiencing today an increasing urgency to help our brothers and sisters, sons and daughters find their respective *Zivug*. Some would argue that this emergency has reached crisis proportions.

Shaya Ostrov, a true Ben Torah, has spent many years counseling singles as well as young couples, and has earned his good reputation among professional and lay people alike. Over the years he has developed a technique which has been used successfully by many. In his new book "The Inner Circle, Seven Gates to Marriage" he shares some of his experiences as well as the "formula" he has developed.

This may indeed be the tool to help many of our future fathers and mothers realize their dreams.

Time constraints have precluded me from reviewing this book. But I am familiar with Reb Shaya and some of his works first hand. I commend him for undertaking such an important project which could prove to be very helpful in our community, where works in this field by Bnei Torah are in short supply.

Yaakov Reisman

Letter of approbation from Rabbi Yaakov Reisman, Shlita
Rav of the Agudath Israel of Far Rockaway

Rabbi Yoel Kramer
Director, Center for Teaching

The problem of the older single in the frum community knocks at the door of every sensitive person. The single feels the never-ending pounding, while family and friends hear the steady tapping. If one doesn't hear any pound they are probably guilty of not listening well enough. But, what to do and how to react?

A major life challenge is balancing logic and emotion. So, too, are we challenged to react to this problem with a balanced approach. Shaya Ostrov walks this tightrope with an incredibly delicate balance. He articulates so sensitively the pathos of the frustrated singles; he is never judgemental and yet, he walks them through logical steps with which to help themselves.

Every single, parents and caring friends will gain enormously from this most readable and sensitive work.

Yoel Kramer

Letter of approbation from Rabbi Yoel Kramer, Shlita

Table of Contents

Introduction 1

I. The Fable of the Seven Gates 12

II. Dating Will Never Be The Same 21

III. I Saw A Chosson Dance 29

IV. The Power of Dating 42

V. Beginning the Journey 65

VI. Introduction To Your Inner Circle 72

VII. Seven Gates to the Kingdom of Marriage 92

    The Critical Focus — Hope And Belief 96

    The Gate of Affirmation 111

    The Gate of Inner History 127

    The Gate of Human Vulnerabilities 137

    The Gate of Caring 147

    The Gate of Transformation - From "I" To "We" . 155

    The Gate of Engagement & Marriage 166

VIII. The Dating Experience 175

IX. The Future of the Inner Circle 202

X. Worksheets 206

XI. Epilogue. 230

Foreword

*I*nvei Hagefen means hope and promise for the thousands of Orthodox single men and women who have devoted their adult lives in search of their Bashert — that one special person who is destined to be their *ezer kenegdo*. Since 1997, Invei Hagefen has worked with Shaya Ostrov as part of our commitment to create a truly effective date mentoring program which could be used by Invei *shadchonim*, professionals and anyone who feels caring and compassionate enough to assist Orthodox singles to find their *zivug*.

We are proud to have played a central role in the development of this program, as it reflects an important milestone in how each of us views singles and, more important, how we go about making a real difference in their lives.

Over the past two years, Mr. Ostrov has worked with Invei *shadchonim* and its board to carefully develop this program, which has already resulted in many singles finding their *bashert*. Many of the couples that you will meet in this volume are actually Invei members who have, *boruch Hashem,* started to create families of their own.

Our work at Invei Hagefen to bring simcha and true personal fulfillment into the lives of countless Orthodox singles has just begun. Through the efforts of our dedicated volunteers and projects such as the Inner Circle – 7 Gates to Marriage, we have created an effective force which will continue to grow, *b'ezras Hashem*, to serve as an example for all *Klal Yisroel*. As a result of these efforts we have developed an organization which demonstrates the power of *mesiras nefesh* to renew hope by transforming lives. Our clear commitment is to pioneer the way for other *shadchonim* and organizations to follow in our footsteps. Our goal is to enable every Orthodox single to experience a life filled with the love, fulfillment, and meaning which *Hashem* has prepared for each of us through the wonderful gift of marriage.

We hope you will learn from and enjoy the many teachings of this volume.

B'vracha
The Invei Hagefen Board

Introduction to the Seven Gates of Marriage

Mature *frum* singles, after years of unsuccessful dating, are painfully aware of the incessant and ceaseless march of time working against them. Regardless of how successful they are in other areas of their lives, marriage remains the one unfulfilled dream which can bring true completion of self. This book is designed to help these mature *frum* singles make every moment count toward that ultimate personal goal of finding their *bashert*. It focuses squarely on successfully developing a relationship which can lead, *b'ezras Hashem* to marriage, and on fulfilling the rich and personally meaningful *mitzvos* related to family life and the future of *Am Yisroel*.

The "Seven Gates" program I have created works dramatically well. Our success rate with *frum* mature singles, ranging in age from thirty to sixty has been beyond all expectations. The program succeeds because it outlines where you're starting from, where you're going and how you're going to get there. While all events lie ultimately in the hands of *hashgocha* (Divine assistance), I like to think of this program as a contribution toward your own *hishtadlus* (committed efforts), which enables *hashgocha* to take place. This is a guide to find your future happiness.

I have one and only one standard of success: marriage. Anything short of marriage is just a prelude to our one concrete goal. While we understand that each dating experience may not turn into marriage, each interpersonal encounter has the potential to bring you closer to understanding how to finally "close the deal," when the right person comes along. Numerous singles, who, though coached through stages of the process, decided not to continue with their dating partners, successfully utilized their new knowledge and insight with their next dating partners.

I have undertaken this project because of my awareness of the ongoing pain and frustration experienced by mature *frum* singles. It has been a challenging and highly rewarding learning experience, enhanced with each successful date and with each *chupah* I have attended. It is precisely because of my awareness of their pain and frustration that this book takes an uncharacteristically challenging stance against many of the shallow and ineffective solutions which pervade and exploit the world of *frum* singles. It pits a disciplined and gradual approach to creating a relationship between two mature adults against the hype of the "must be there mixers," unforgettable weekends, stimulating lectures, meaningful and experiential workshops, insight evoking personal counseling sessions, vacations, cruises and on and on. Each of these are legitimate activities in their own right, particularly as they succeed in filling time, fighting boredom and warding off loneliness. However, from the growing number of singles populating our landscape, these activities can hardly claim any serious success stories leading to marriage. Without a proven concrete program which can consistently help dating singles move their relationship forward, these activities only help professional organizers live off the fat of that wonderful disposable income for which singles are so well known.

This program succeeds by creating delicately woven moments of bonding between two people. Since 1973, my practice of marital and family therapy has consistently taught me that meaningful encounters between two people have the potential to transform realities to recreate new and wonderful beginnings. As I invested more of my time to help mature singles marry, I began to understand that for the overwhelming majority, the key to success was not in the professional counseling office or workshops, but what happens between them on the actual date, where these meaningful moments may need to be carefully crafted. Together, we learned that dates are potentially precious events holding the possibility of developing that one special relationship, more precious than all others. Dates should never be "thrown away" or misused by following an old script which has failed time and again. A successful date holds no wasted moment, from the first phone call to the farewell at the date's end.

I learned that the focus on a date had to be from the internal side of our personalities, the *pnimius,* rather than the external, social and superficial dimension of who we are. Through this focus on the *pnimius* dimension, meaningful relationships are evoked throughout the dating experience. It's this focus which is crucial in the search for that one special person destined to be your life partner. This focus on the *pnimius* is called your Inner Circle. Once you have discovered your own precious and very personal Inner Circle, my program takes you progressively through seven gates toward marriage. Each date and moment then becomes a carefully focused step toward your goal.

This book is divided into three essential sections. The first section deals with an analysis of those forces which keep mature Frum singles alone and unsuccessful in their search for their *bashert.* It explores the dynamics which deprive them of a level playing field, stacking the odds hopelessly against their success at marriage. The second section defines the focus, the Inner Circle, and the seven stages toward marriage. The last section brings you through the dating process from beginning to end.

≈ *This Road Map is Not A Theory*

This book is a road map. I don't offer readers my theories, which may be wonderful for academicians, but lacking for mature *frum* singles. Their need to marry is far too compelling to find solace and solutions in well phrased ideas. I have aspired to create a volume which can be used as a road map, to tell you when to begin your journey and how to continue on your destination. Along the way you'll stop to check that you're not heading toward a dead end, or even on a six lane beautifully designed cloverleaf superhighway that gives you an illusion of speed, but leads you in circles until you run out of gas. Some people always seem to have the accelerator pedal to the floor. They're dating continuously, one after the next. The only problem is that they're in neutral, making noise and movement with no progress. Progress toward marriage, to maintain that focus and achieve that goal, are my only measures of success.

On an emotional level, each gate signifies a distinct and separate set of experiences specific to that stage. Each stage presents its own unique challenge. My role is to keep you in a relationship feeling balanced and in control of your life with a clear understanding of what is happening within yourself, your dating partner and in the relationship at each specific stage.

≑ *A Message to Mature Singles:*

Throughout this book, I will be sharing with you my experiences — both successes and frustrations — at helping other singles marry. But my final message is clear. Unlike the painful experiences of far too many mature singles today, the journey I am offering toward marriage is not long, arduous and exhausting. The road I have paved, guides you toward a growing sense of closeness and emotional intimacy leading to mutual caring, commitment and marriage. The true challenge of the journey is in your ability to adopt new attitudes about how you date. It requires you to maintain a clear focus while steadily progressing from one level of a relationship to the next. If you read the material carefully and integrate these concepts and skills in the way you date and communicate, then this book will provide you with a new and exciting tool to bring you closer to marriage.

☙ *My Responsibility and Your Responsibility*

Each gate makes emotional demands on you. You will be asked to take calculated risks toward solidifying a relationship. In the 4th gate you will be asked to share an aspect of your personal frailties. I call this The Gate Of Human Vulnerability. This sharing is a way of creating an opportunity for your dating partner to demonstrate an ability to be protective, though you may feel it is an opportunity for this person to feel strength and power over you. These are the defining moments which determine the life and future of your relationship. My responsibility is to guide you through this "staged" sharing of vulnerability. It leads to surprising results, deepening and solidifying your relationship. Your responsibility is to follow each task as precisely as possible. Every task you will be asked to do has been successfully used with others and has clearly demonstrated its value but only when carefully followed. You will find that each gate will lead to many surprises, a sense of exhilaration and stimulation. As a result, along the way you will begin to feel a renewed sense of hope and emotional commitment to the promise of life together with a person who deeply cares for you. My goal is to guide each one of you along this path through the seven gates to a marriage that will last a lifetime and create future generations who will stand up to eternity.

≑ *You Will Need a Mentor*

This program was never meant to be a self help guide. With every important step in life we require guidance. No one can take a new journey alone. This program will require you to enter into new and challenging interpersonal experiences with your dating partner in an effort to determine whether this person really is your *bashert*. This book provides you the direction and even the scripts to initiate these experiences. However, to succeed, you will need a mentor to guide you along and keep you on track. This mentor can be a friend, a *shadchon*, or a trained mentor to shepherd you through each stage. Your mentor will be helpful in crafting your dating preparations and in helping you review the results of your focused dates. Invei Hagefen has initiated a mentor training program for Invei volunteers. I believe that anyone who has read and integrated the concepts of this book can serve a productive role in mentoring a friend or a client toward steady progress.

≋ Behind The Mask of our Couples

The material selected in this book is a chronicle of events which have unfolded over the past two years in my work with mature singles. Names, genders and ages of the people in this book have been disguised to ensure anonymity. I have attempted to stay as faithful as possible to the nuances and the nature of the relationships which make each of these stories unique and important in helping other mature singles use these principles in their own lives. Be assured, each vignette and anecdote is solidly based on true dating experiences.

≋ My Appreciation

The development of this program began a number of years ago through Rabbi and Mrs. Dovid Greenblatt and Mrs. Leah Hellman, who have devoted so much of their lives to helping mature singles. My initial exposure to their selfless efforts left me inspired enough to take the issue seriously. Through Rabbi Yoel Kramer, Rabbi Nisson Wolpin and Mrs. Hannah Parness, I undertook the program's first steps by working together with Invei Hagefen, the Agudah sponsored organization for mature singles. As a result of the efforts of Mrs. Leah Gelernter and her dedicated colleagues of volunteers who work together so tirelessly at Invei, the initial workshop series enabled us to secure a serious forum to test out new ideas and approaches. Invei consistently provided an invaluable source of support and resources, including Mrs. Pessie Schwartz of the Invei office. The commitment and ongoing dedication of Invei's board members, including Yatti Weinreb, Mendy Zilberberg and Rabbi Yoel Kramer enabled me to stay focused on the task at hand.

In addition, two social work professionals, Shaya Lebovitz and Ayelet Mellman, provided me with much needed initial encouragement and assistance. I must also give mention to my two *chavrusos*, Yisroel Bloom and Yehudah Wurtzel, whose personal commitment to this issue and weekly Shabbos feedback were essential in the evolution of this program. Mrs. Liba Leiberman was extremely helpful and creative in applying her much needed critical editing skills to the manuscripts to achieve a product worthy of publishing. And my warmest gratitude to Rachel Slamovits who has continuously volunteered her time to assist me in editing and preparing material at different stages of its long development, starting with the initial drafts almost two years ago. My dearest niece, Laura Ostrov, generously gave of her precious time to prepare the manuscript for its final form. My esteemed friend and colleague, Dr. Dovid Steiner, assisted me with the final draft by offering invaluable suggestions and constructively critical insights. I thank you all. I want to publicly express my friendship and gratitude to my colleagues and partners who I work with and see on a daily basis and who unfailingly demonstrate their friendship and support my efforts. Each is a *baal chesed* and a profound *mentch*, Dovid, Boruch and Meir. I wish them *hatzlocha* and pray that *siyata d'shmaya* will guide them and protect them in all areas of their lives. Finally, the last touches and masterful graphics and layout were prepared by the tireless and talented hands of Avrohom Kay.

If any one person has been my lynch pin of support in nurturing the development of this program, it has been my beloved wife of almost thirty three years, Vivian. This program took over two years to develop. It grew from an inspiring idea into a successful reality without the benefit of financial support or revenues. There were deep financial sacrifices and countless days away from home providing workshops, as well as endless phone calls from the steady stream of singles. At every stage, Vivian was there to encourage, understand and contribute her *kochos* to the final successful outcome. Without her support and encouragement, this program and the marriages they have thus far helped to build would never have been possible. Now, through her encouragement and the assistance of all those who have contributed their time and talents, we have a gift and a dream to offer to each and every mature single.

My last expression of gratitude is actually my first. It is to Hashem who has lovingly guided me throughout my life and rewarded me with greater *chasodim* than I could ever imagine or deserve. The greatest gift of all, however, is how He has enabled me to discover that it is possible to turn what was initially life's greatest hurt and pain into golden *brochos* for myself, my family and others.

≋ My Tefillah

I pray to *Hashem* that the insights and experiences portrayed in this book will create shared moments of interpersonal magic, over and over between couples who were once separate, strangers and apart. And that these once separate individuals will come to share the *simcha* and *mitzvos* of love, marriage and family life with each other and all *Klal Yisroel*.

I. The Fable of the Seven Gates

♆ *Introduction to the Fable*

Before I start I'd like to present an overview of the pathways you will be taking in reading this book. I believe the best way to achieve this is through a fable. The fable symbolizes each element of my program. If you feel uncomfortable groping in the dark for its meaning you have my whole-hearted permission to first read the interpretation and then go back to read the fable. The fable is presented from the perspective of a prince, but is equally applicable to a princess.

I. THE FABLE OF THE SEVEN GATES

◈ *The Fable*

There once lived a beloved king who ruled his kingdom with benevolence and wisdom, just as his father had done, his grandfather and so many generations before him. This king had an only son whom he loved dearly. As was his family tradition, he began grooming the prince early in life to assume the mantle of royalty. To be crowned, the prince had to follow a centuries old ritual which was performed by all his predecessors. This ritual to assume the throne required that the prince win the hand of a princess, groomed from her early years to assume the role of queen. But to win her hand, the prince had to pass through seven gates of love and wisdom.

At the center of the kingdom, lay a royal pond surrounded by blossoming trees, the vibrant colors of which gently shimmered upon the pond's tranquil waters. The young prince would walk along the path around the royal pond and pass through seven gates. At each gate he would stop, take a small precious jewel, cast it into the royal pond and then watch the ripples form on the still surface of the water. If he was wise and loving enough to pass through the gate, the ripples he created would weave a magical story of love between the prince and his princess. When the story had been woven on the surface of the pond he knew that he had successfully passed through the gate. Once he had passed through each of the seven gates, his prize would be the hand of his princess. Together they would rule the kingdom and the subjects would rejoice over their new monarchs.

The role of the king was to tutor his son in the secrets of casting the jewels at each gate, and then deciphering the tale of love and wisdom as told by the gently forming ripples in the royal pond. This king was very proud of his son. "My son, I wait for the day that you will pass through the seven gates and remove the crown from my head. You will then wear it on yours. This will be happiest day of my life."

The young prince grew in stature, wisdom and love for his people. Suddenly, the king took ill. He said to his son. "My dear prince, I am ill and you must assume the responsibilities of state before either you or I had intended. You must pass through the seven gates as soon as possible." The son replied,

"Father, I am not ready, I am just learning the secrets of love and wisdom."

Then tragedy struck and the beloved king died.

The young prince was broken. He could not bear to continue life without his father. Even more so, he was unprepared for the challenge of the seven gates. In his despair and hopelessness he left the palace one night and ran as far as his young legs would take him. He ran off to a land where no one knew of him or his father.

Years passed by and the young boy grew, not in the ways of royalty, but in the ways of peasants. He was now a young man of the land, yet he was haunted by the thoughts of the kingdom he left behind. He thought of returning, however he believed he could never pass through the seven gates and learn the ancient art of listening to and observing the tale of love as told by the gentle ripples in the pond. Sadly, he resigned himself to remaining a lonely peasant for the remainder of his life.

The prince's mind and heart continued to long for his

I. THE FABLE OF THE SEVEN GATES

kingdom, his people, his princess and his castle. He decided to visit his kingdom, just to see the land, the people and the castle that was once his home. There was no need to disguise himself. He was now a scruffy peasant and did not possess the aristocratic bearing he once carried so naturally.

He traveled over the mountains and after many months arrived at his land. Everywhere he went, on the farms, at the marketplaces, at the small villages, he found saddened people. He would always ask "Why are you so sad?"

The answer was always the same "We are a kingdom without a king and queen. Our castle is empty and it shall stay that way until it is occupied by its rightful and beloved monarchs." Then he went past the home of the princess who had been appointed to be his queen. He observed her from afar. She was lovely and fair and from the distance he observed that she too was sad. He understood her sadness without asking.

Deeply moved by the answers of his subjects and the sight of his forlorn princess, he was overcome by a desire to assume the role that was rightfully and morally his. But how could he achieve this without his father's wisdom?

He made his way to the abandoned castle. There he camped outside for many days and prayed with a pained heart and eyes overflowing with tears: "Dear Lord of the universe, this kingdom and my princess await me. How can I pass through the seven gates of wisdom and love to win the hand of my princess and claim my kingdom?"

After many days of prayer he fell into a deep sleep. In his sleep he dreamed he was walking along the trail of the royal pond. From the distance he could see his father approaching him, holding a velvet bag filled with the special jewels.

"My son, you have returned to rule the kingdom which awaits you. These are the jewels to cast into the royal pond.

Stay by this castle and every day I will visit you until you grow in wisdom, love and inner strength. Stay here and I will guide you through each of the seven gates." The prince awoke, startled to realize it was a dream. Was it a fantasy or had he actually been visited by his late father? At his side he discovered the velvet bag of jewels. He lifted them up and gazed at them in all their sparkling beauty. A miracle had occurred. Hope filled his heart. He now believed that the throne would be his.

Every day, the young prince returned to the castle where he grew in the wisdom and understanding required to pass through each of the gates. When he was ready, he revealed himself to the elders of the kingdom. Having exchanged his peasant's clothing and groomed himself as a prince, the elders immediately recognized the young prince they had once known so well. They were overjoyed. They then asked him the inevitable question: could he pass through the seven gates of wisdom and love? Did he possess the precious jewels? And did he know the secret to understanding the ripples of love and wisdom shimmering on the surface of the royal pond?

Together with the elders he walked confidently along the path of the royal pond. At each gate, the young prince drew upon the teachings of his father. At each gate he approached the pond, carefully took a precious jewel and cast it gently into the silent and quiet waters. With each jewel the pond shimmered with a magical story and song of love. Finally, he reached the final gate. The kingdom rejoiced. Accompanied by the elders and a royal entourage, he made his way to the home of the princess to claim her hand. The young prince felt the presence of his father, the king.

He closed his eyes and whispered: "Dear father, thank you for your gift of love and wisdom."

At last they were husband and wife, king and queen. At last the kingdom had a royal couple to rule them. At last an empty castle was now filled with life and love. Together they would rule the kingdom — the kingdom of marriage.

≑ Symbolism Of The Fable

This fable and its symbols are metaphors for the way marriage is seen in Jewish life. The kingdom is marriage itself. The empty castle is the home which awaits its future king and queen — our bride and groom. The seven gates are seven stages of a relationship which lead to marriage. Each stage requires its own level of maturity, mutual growth and a deepening sense of love and understanding. The saddened citizens of the kingdom are generations, past, present and even future for whom your happiness, fulfillment and ability to create a marriage and family mean very much. They share in and feel your sense of emptiness and incompleteness. The king represents your Inner Circle. These are your many teachers in life who have and will continue to guide you with knowledge and direction to bring you successfully through each of the seven stages of a relationship and on to marriage.

What are these jewels in the pond and the enchanted songs of its ripples? The jewels are those messages and questions you will share with your date. These are not superficial thoughts, but penetrating and meaningful ideas which communicate with the heart of a person and create a dramatic impact. Your jewels create ripples — the gentle effects created by your words and actions to create a special relationship. In time, as you carefully follow the lessons of this book, you will learn to understand the subtle and gentle language of these ripples, these deeply personal responses, and successfully pass through each of the seven gates. Each gate will bring you closer to your *bashert* until you reach the hand of your princess, or prince, to rule in the kingdom of marriage.

≉ *Three Pillars Which Create The Bond:*

1: Living Means Growing

Our prince does not fall in love. He grows in love and wisdom through each of the seven gates. The first pillar of this program states that all relationships must grow and evolve from one stage to the next. Relationships are like all organic growth in life. Trees and plants follow a divine blueprint for their development, as does the growth of the human fetus and even the spiritual development in each of us. They all follow progressive stages. That's why there are 49 days between Pesach and Shevuos. We all need time to grow from one level to the next. It's the same with a loving relationship which leads to marriage. There have to be stages. One stage must follow the next as a relationship grows between two people, until it's strong enough to create the bond of marriage. This program provides seven stages. Learning them and understanding how to use them will bring you closer to marriage.

2: If You Want to Take Charge Get Focused

The second pillar in this program is that the prince is clearly focused on his treasured goal of marriage to his *bashert*. Once he has guidance and direction, nothing deters him. If two people are uncertain, each pursuing an unclear and blind path, then marriage is a very long shot, regardless of how well suited the couple is for each other. The second pillar of this program states that someone needs a clear and uninterrupted focus, clearly set on how to move a relationship forward from its initial stages all the way through to engagement. This program will teach many of you how to focus, what to focus on, and how to maintain that focus.

3: Become A Creator of Ripples

The last principle which our prince learns is that he must become a master at deciphering the ripples of love and wisdom. He must become an artist who can understand the stirrings of his princess' heart. With the foundation in place, armed with a clear road map, you can then open pathways to new levels in a relationship. These pathways are based on a greater capacity for giving, sharing and personal understanding to create gentle ripples in the hearts of someone you are trying to speak to emotionally through your gifts of caring and understanding. At first, you may not see or be aware of the ripples you create, but in time you will begin to recognize the emotional responses to your gifts, your jewels, which you have gently dropped into the pond of this person's life and consciousness. You will learn to be sensitive to and decipher the language of these ripples. You will learn to communicate with another person through songs of love and wisdom, shared privately between two people searching for a life together. This is how you will bring your relationship forward, continuously growing toward the promise of love and sharing a life of fulfillment together. In the end, it is my deepest wish that you will be richly rewarded with the keys to the kingdom.

II. Dating Will Never Be the Same

❧ The Sweet Taste Of Success

The fable explains that to create a relationship leading to marriage, the prince must walk down the royal path through each of the seven gates. These gates are the same for everyone. You need to acquire the knowledge and skills that will carry you all the way from that first phone call to the *chupah*. Lack of focus inevitably leads to confusion, helplessness and doubt and stops relationships dead in their tracks before they can grow.

Your goal is to replicate a feeling of confidence and competence in dating, similar to participating in a professional meeting, a *shiur* or volunteering your services. You want to feel that sense of " I know what I'm doing." As a child I remember being a terrible baseball player who never managed to hit a ball out of the infield. Mostly I struck out. I was about twelve years old and was a resident in a convalescent home recovering from a childhood illness. In this convalescent home, the key to success was hitting a baseball. If you could hit, you were chosen into the game. If you were chosen, you were accepted. If not, you were a scapegoat and on the receiving end of ridicule. Being away from home and sickly made the hurt of my failure at baseball very painful. Every swing of the bat was an exercise in utter defeat. I saw myself as an inferior person, and as a failure.

One day, a counselor, who had obviously been watching me from the sidelines and was moved by the pitiful sight of an undersized kid missing everything in sight, came over to me. He quietly positioned himself at my side, gently lifting my shoulders, saying: "You'll be all right. You just have to swing level and straight."

I felt his reassurance. He proceeded to guide my arms to swing, as if I were hitting the ball. Together we practiced a slow methodical swing of the bat. I felt good about his concern and the instruction. Inside, I asked myself: "What difference does it make, same ball, same bat, same me?" After three or four practice swings he sent me back up to the plate and reminded me one more time: "Just remember, keep your shoulders up, swing level and straight." The ball came toward me, I picked up my shoulders to make sure they were straight. My arms started the swing. I felt contact. It was hard and sweet. I'll never forget the feeling of solid impact with that ball. I watched in amazement as it soared in an almost straight trajectory to the outfield. I had never hit a ball so far in my life. There was no greater effort, no stronger swing. Same me, same bat, same ball. I tried it again and hit the ball just as far. I wanted to start dancing on that ball field. I experienced a great personal victory which I can still taste four decades later.

I learned a lesson that day which I never forgot: I could have stayed at that plate swinging at air forever and nothing would have changed. Without guidance we seem to always make the same mistakes. But when someone guides you, holds up your shoulders straight and steady, then you can correct your mistakes. And doing something right delivers a sweet taste of mastery and usually ends in success. It's a brand new experience, bearing no relationship whatsoever to past attempts which have repeatedly failed. The key is for someone to be there, to guide and direct you from beginning to end. This is the same for a fabled prince seeking guidance on a royal path, a small kid trying to hit a ball in a big way, or a mature single attempting to turn a life experience with failed dates into marriage. This is my goal for you — to help you date with a sense of clear direction. The most important goal is to free you of the old mistakes and misconceptions which get repeated date after date, leaving you swinging at air and feeling very defeated.

In being guided through each stage of this program you will master a sense of emotional achievement and understand what it means to get close to another person- step by step. Growth in life always requires new stages.

We see this in a child learning to walk, talk, give, share and grow into a mature adult. All growth requires guidance. This is true in all human relationships, especially marriage. This book will serve as your map and guide, step by step.

≆ *The Energy Source of Marriage*

To move from one point to the next on the emotional map you need a fuel source strong enough to propel you to the finish line. Marriage doesn't spring out of spontaneous generation. It is fueled by the same internal drive which *Hashem* placed in *Odom* and *Chava*. This drive to discover your *bashert*, your *ezer kenegdo*, is what moves you toward marriage. It is a continuous inner drive, streaming outward, searching continuously to create deep and penetrating emotional connections with one precious human being. These sparks created between two lives develop into trust and a desire for the permanence and security of marriage.

In the biological world, energy comes from light, heat, chemical and physical reactions, all Divinely guided to create life. The world of *ruchnius* is fueled by an inner spark of life, seeking *shlaimus* — completion — as a fundamental requirement which links us to the source and meaning of existence. In the world of marriage, the sparks which fuel our relationship are the desire between two people for shared moments which create an interpersonal bond that can last a lifetime. Life is filled with other motivations bringing two people together such as sensual, social and even financial drives. But mature singles have been through too much to settle for anything less than that unquestionably pure relationship in which they feel their lives were destined to share. After years of searching, their understanding of life has taken on a deeper perspective and now requires a more profound connection.

Maturation leads to greater insight, and the mature single yearns for the deeper connections. These connections, however, just don't emerge, any more than a casual jogger can jump overnight from his usual 2.5 mile jog to a twenty-six mile marathon. Stamina, endurance, muscle strength and even the ability to stay mentally alert all require gradual increments over time. Because they are mature and experienced they sense that they know what a relationship worthy of marriage should be, and will settle for nothing less. Yet, because they don't have a clue as to how to move from their 2.5 mile limit to the twenty-six miles required to complete the marathon, they find themselves continuously stuck and unable to realize their dreams of finding that one special person. They can not bring themselves to marry for superficial reasons. Too much has been given up along the years of being alone. Their dreams of their *bashert* become lofty, and their investment in their lifestyles intensify. This is why so many lives are passing without marriage. And as their lives move on without finding their marriage partner, singles learn that to survive they must continuously protect themselves by reinforcing their lifestyle with all the social, professional and financial support required to keep the ship afloat. Therefore, when a single individual reaches beyond the thirties and forties and older, lifestyle and self become integrally connected. They may very much want to marry. At the same time, they also want very much not to change what has given them comfort and protection.

The result is that the idea that marriage can really occur becomes more remote and difficult to believe in. So many mature singles harbor unfulfilled romantic dreams impossible to fill. Love and marriage seem to only happen to the young. They look to younger singles who apparently find "instant love," which becomes a standard for being swept off your feet. I have heard many such people say: "If I don't feel that special connection right from the first moment, those first few seconds, I know it's going nowhere." What many mature singles fail to understand is that for younger singles marriage is easier to commit to because their lifestyle has yet to evolve and therefore, they have less to protect. Marriage of the young takes on a "fairy tale" quality, because it is easier for them to make a commitment to each other when their lives have yet to be filled by other commitments. The young couple are all too willing and ready to leave the homes of their childhood and build a new one together.

By contrast, older singles have made great personal investments in their life style. It's not so easy to give away the security and independence fought for so dearly. IRAs become more valuable, apartments increase in value, job security become more important. The ability to come and go without checking in or out with someone becomes the given. The social commitments become more intense.

Therefore, to make room in their lives for another person, deep and powerful connections have to gradually and progressively grow. These connections have to be more promising and meaningful than anything else in their lives. They have to achieve the seemingly impossible and become more promising and significant than professional growth, personal savings, family and social commitments. Marriage becomes a reality when shared moments have the power to transform mature singles into mature couples and connect two people in a joined emotional union as deep as the ocean.

≋ *Seven Gates To Marriage*

As in the fable, the path on which all are embarking will take you on a journey through the seven gates leading to marriage. Because growth always occurs in progressive and orderly stages, each stage is designed to follow the previous one.

The seven gates you will proceed through are:

1. Focus on Hope and Belief
2. Affirmations
3. The Inner History
4. Human Vulnerability
5. Caring
6. Inner Transformation- From "I" To "We"
7. Engagement and Marriage

≋ *To Summarize*

My goal is to help you find inspiration and success through a step by step approach which moves you from the very beginning of a relationship on through marriage. These shared experiences of trust, understanding and mutual nurturance, all combine to result in emerging feelings of certainty that love can indeed occur in your lives. Each level requires a very conscious effort on your part to integrate these experiences into your consciousness and behavior. You are not just changing with this person alone. Your understanding of all significant relationships is affected by what you are learning. By using this new way of seeing the world, you can be strong enough to stand up to the pulls and counter-pressures generated by the commitments and comforts which are so much a part of your single life style. This is how you move on toward marriage.

This book, if properly used, will make dating a new experience for each of you. I suggest you not only start looking for new dates but also consider calling on former dating partners where there was once a potential to develop a relationship. I'll describe how to contact former dates in the section devoted to Selecting A Date. The guiding principle is that if the feeling and potential was once there, it makes sense to try it again using the methods you'll be learning in this book.

III. I Saw a Chosson Dance

I Saw A Chosson Dance
I Saw A Gift Of Life Unfolding

I recently attended the wedding of a couple I had been working with and was moved to record the following impressions:

> *I saw a Chosson dance with unabashed and uninhibited*
> *joy before his Kallah.*
> *He danced with greater pleasure and laughter than I can*
> *ever remember.*
> *He slapped his thighs and stomped his feet.*
> *His simcha became our simcha as we all danced around him.*

*I watched his Kallah gaze upon him as he
sang "Eishes Chayil."
A soft glistening tear gently, silently,
rolling down her cheek.
Her joy was private and subdued.
I now understood a deeper meaning of:
"Kol Kevoda Bas Melech Penima."
"Great is the honor of the modest princess."*

*We danced and our hearts overflowed for this
Chosson and Kallah.
They were not ordinary.
They were older, more mature,
beyond their 40s
They were marrying for the first time.
Many of us who came to dance doubted
we would ever be a part of this wedding.
Now their two lives had become surprisingly
and magically intertwined.
Elated and deeply moved, we all knew we
were witnesses
to a gift of life unfolding.
A gift of life and love unfolding before our
eyes and hearts.*

*Such is the Simcha when two mature singles,
who have spent so many difficult years alone
and apart, are now Chosson and Kallah.
They can now start life again.
This is the theme and purpose of this book.*

III. I SAW A CHOSSON DANCE

≎ *A New Approach To Dating*

I felt a part of this wedding. I was deeply moved by an inspiring and elevating "thought." These two people were brought together under the *chupah* at this stage of their lives by their ability to create and share special moments together. Rachel had participated in a workshop on dating, communications and relationships, provided to older singles. But it wasn't the workshop which made a difference. It was what happened afterward.

In many ways, Rachel was responsible for helping me shift from presenting workshops to designing a program which focused on "real time" dating skills. The workshops made great sense, but when they were over I received calls asking: "What do I do now?" "Walking" Rachel through her dates with David, I discovered that dates between mature singles, which frequently lead nowhere, had the potential to become a powerhouse of unforgettable emotional exchanges. From date to date we were able to identify new stages of caring and openness. By following prescribed tasks, advice and direction had a way of creating powerful ripples in the relationship. I witnessed them joining together in a remarkable bond that neither had experienced before in their lives. The potential was always there. It was simply untapped.

≎ *Triumph Over Doubt*

While at their wedding I sat down to record the impact of his dancing and her quiet tears, because their triumph had to be chronicled and shared, for themselves and countless others like them. Rachel and David were now Chosson and (his) Kallah. Both had struggled with loneliness and disappointment over countless years of dating. Both persisted and continued to believe in and search for that one person. When it finally happened, Rachel wrote David: "it's a Ness (a miracle)." A ness is when what once seemed impossible, somehow, becomes a reality.

Their dating started as many other dates in the past. A mutual friend suggested the possibility of their getting together. They went out a few times. Past experiences left them both wary and cautious about not to expect too much. The beginning was easy. They were amiable, friendly and socially compatible enough to say: "We'll wait and see." They found friendship in each other and were even physically attracted to each other. The beginning of their dating seemed promising. There were even far off and distant dreams of "perhaps this is the person I have been waiting for."

As their dating continued, they both felt a need to relate on a deeper level. A more serious commitment required more in-depth knowledge and insight between them. More serious considerations of marriage required Rachel to feel something for David that she doubted could ever evolve. In short, each side was waiting for something extraordinary to happen. She soon was ready to end the relationship, as she had with others in the past. This was the point at which Rachel called me.

Rachel's history was consistent: while dating, this was the point where things always seemed to dry up. She couldn't see herself marrying a man who was unable to open up. While on a superficial level, so many elements seemed right, she questioned proceeding with a partner who didn't have the ability to show depth and feelings in a relationship. This is where hesitation took hold and the doubts deepened. They continued to date, but inside, their relationship was unraveling- against her own deeper wishes and desire to continue. With each passing day she was becoming increasingly ready to say goodbye. A relationship that had potential was rapidly dying, and with it, hopes and dreams.

I understood that Rachel was unique, but also carrying the same dilemma as so many other mature singles I had known. How can we ask her to marry someone for whom she had no deep feelings? The patterns of Rachel's past were being repeating once again as it had with so many other opportunities for marriage. On the one hand, here was a person, honest and caring, deeply yearning for a soul mate, deeply committed to making this relationship work. Doubts were taking hold and the opportunity began to slip away. She felt helpless to save what appeared, for a while, to be so promising.

Rachel and David are real. They are also a prototype of so many other couples. They represent the sincerity, the commitment, the determination, along with the helplessness to bring a dating relationship to a level where each says: "I can now say, with a full and complete heart that I can marry you." The result was that Rachel was filled now with doubt over a relationship that had once felt promising. She was also honestly "relieved" that she wasn't entering into a relationship which could not fulfill her basic needs for emotional honesty and openness. Rachel was too frightened to leave the relationship and had no idea how to proceed to make it real enough to consider marriage. Her greatest fear was that it would continue and go nowhere. When she turned to me it was out of utter desperation and a feeling that things could never be resolved.

This became the initial setting and background in which I worked with a couple to use dates to create meaningful and powerful moments. The give and take between these two people over the next two months demonstrated a couple's super-human capacity for love, emotional honesty, nurturance and very creative damage control during crises. All of this led to the *chupah*. It was an exhilarating, although at times worrisome, journey for them as well as myself.

≅ *Challenge To The Life Style*

The Davids and Rachels of the world all want very much to marry, but are mysteriously unable to move forward. What prevents them from feeling secure and certain enough to marry? What stops them cold in their tracks after dating for months, and in some instances even years, with the same person?

The answer to the contradiction may be in the pulls and commitments of their lives. When two mature, unmarried people have led independent lives for so many years they are also wise and intelligent enough to understand that since marriage and family hasn't happened, they had better protect themselves by leading balanced and productive lives through creating a self sufficient and independent life style. The results is that mature singles develop their lives on two almost contradictory levels. On one level there is the ever present dream and longing to marry and have a family, live together in companionship and belonging with a person they deeply love. Even if they forget the dream during the week, it's rekindled every Shabbos and Yom Tov. There is just no escaping the "missing" person in their lives.

On another level, the stark realities of survival in urban life, along with the painful and frustrating experiences of the past attempts to find their *bashert*, are convincing reasons to create an independent life which sustains and protects them from the loneliness and frustration inherent in being a mature single. The result is that singles inevitably must create a lifestyle of dignity and self respect which has to be protected. They work hard and seriously at holding on to friends, affiliations, professional advancement, commitment to parents and family members. Maintaining this lifestyle becomes an important investment. It's preserving and protecting, both emotionally and socially, in a world where they are deprived of such basic and fundamental relationships as acceptance in the general community, children, and of course, a marriage partner.

One young woman said to me: "Sure, I want to get married. Very much so. But, it's hard to make room, unless I'm absolutely sure he's perfect for me. If someone comes along, my attitude has become, he has to fit into my life. Because at this stage I don't want to have to choose between what I know works for me and what is essentially a question mark." So, as years pass and marriage still hasn't come, the absence of marriage is accompanied by strengthening commitments to a single life style.

Along with these two realities, a deeper and fundamental doubt sets in as to whether there really is anyone out there who can be all they had hoped to find after all these years of searching. I am not clairvoyant and can't peer into anyone's soul. However, we all have to consider the question: to what degree is the doubt about ever getting married rooted in a deepening entrenchment of the single lifestyle and emotional commitments to job, family and friends? Along with this is the question: to what degree is marriage held at bay by a sense of hopelessness that what has not occurred until now will probably never happen?

My answer can only be that hopelessness and a fortification of the "singles" lifestyle may very well feed on each other. The result is that marriage appears to become increasingly remote as the single now has to be convinced that the relationship being developed must be able to provide all the emotional, psychological, physical and financial rewards which they presently experience in their lives, even though marriage and family are absent. And while being single certainly isn't marriage, it is difficult to give up what has been created so thoughtfully and carefully over the years, for a relationship which may wind up in even greater pain and loss.

⚜ *The Emotional Challenge*

Another challenge to the mature single is that years of dating and searching inevitably leave their emotional toll. With each failed attempt scars remain. A very wise rabbi once said in Yiddish that when it comes to *shidduchim* *"mir gebben klap und mir kriggen klap."* (We give our licks and we take licks.) Finding a marriage partner is serious business and it can be a battlefield with casualties. Particularly when the soldiers have been "out there" for so many years. So, while there may still be a serious desire and yearning to find that one special person, there is also the very frightening thought of emotionally taking another chance.

I have a friend who has been successfully in business for many years. Recently he told me that he's tired and worn out from closing business deals. He says: "I've been out there too many years. I hacked away and got hacked at. Now I'm tired. The idea of starting any more deals is just too much." The battle has worn him down. What happens when success is elusive, if there is any to speak of at all?

Sarah is a thirty year old former Bais Yaakov student and now an accomplished computer programmer. Since she started dating almost a decade ago she has dated countless young men. At first she dated seriously. She was even willing to consider men who she realized represented a compromise for her. She was determined to marry. Yet, every attempt failed and in the process of a decade she now feels tired and scarred. The more she dates, the more distant she feels from her dating partners. She views her dates as increasingly infantile, self absorbed and too involved in their professions and pursuit of wealth. She has decided that it makes more sense to spend time with her female single friends instead of dating men. For her, a *Motzie Shabbos* is far more comfortable when spent with close female friends, and certainly more fun than with a date. Men and *shadchonim* continue to call. But, she has essentially stopped dating. "If something really special comes along I'll consider going out."

For Sarah, refusing to date is an act of self preservation. For her parents, her future as a potential wife and mother and for all *Klal Yisroel,* this is an unmitigated tragedy. Sarah is a human being with feelings and emotional limits. I believe she has gone past her threshold for pain and disappointment. The reality hasn't changed. Her hurt and her doubts deepened, date by failed date. This is what changed her perceptions. Now Sarah waits home for her ideal date, or there is no date. The more hopeless she feels, the more concrete and inflexible she has become. "I've had enough!"

≉ *Expectations Of Perfection*

Recently, an acquaintance, Bracha, who spends much of her time volunteering to help singles, acted as a Shadchon for an old friend, Miriam, a thirty-four year old single. Miriam has been watching the clock tick away and feeling increasingly hopeless about ever getting married. Bracha set up a date for her. The couple went out, and Miriam didn't call with any feedback. The fellow called, and was willing to go out again. But nothing was heard from Miriam.

It took about a week for Bracha to make contact with Miriam. Bracha was hurt and felt slighted. She had worked hard on getting Miriam the date and Miriam never called back. When she finally spoke to Miriam,

Bracha managed to hold in her disappointment and asked: "How close was that fellow I set you up with to what you were looking for?"

Miriam was unaware of Bracha's feelings and expectations that she should have called back. She felt justified in not responding, because the date was a nonstarter which didn't meet her expectations.

"I appreciate the effort, Bracha. But when you throw someone a life preserver who is drowning and it lands one hundred feet away, does it make a difference whether or not it's close? It just makes no difference."

Brocha knew that the answer reflected Miriam seeing herself as going under for the third time. The women are old friends. Bracha was hurt, but knew enough about Miriam's desperation not to take the answer personally.

I don't believe that Miriam is really drowning. Her need for a perfectly placed life preserver is influenced by her feelings of helplessness. With greater mastery she can have the ability to feel more hopeful, see greater possibilities and find creative approaches to work on relationships which can lead to marriage.

Recently, I received a call from Asher, asking me to help him find a date. He finished the conversation with: "I'm already forty-four, I've already wasted too much time. So if you can't find me exactly what I'm looking for, please don't bother to try." At first, I was put off by his reaction. Then I remembered what took me so long to understand: the greater the desperation, the greater the inflexibility.

Asher is in many ways like Miriam. The older he gets, the more hopeless he feels, and the more precise he is in defining his perception of his ideal dating partner. But desperation can never define the qualities of the person you want to marry. People are never what they "appear" to be. Their true personality and depth can only emerge under the right conditions. On an inner level, both Miriam and Asher are missing something. Neither understands that the people they date also have an inner life, a force waiting to be tapped. Your first impression makes no difference, because it has no relationship to the true reality of the person you are dating. Each person possesses an underlying energy that can emerge through the right dating experience.

☙ *Path To An Enduring Relationship*

With these elements in place, we can take a bit of a closer look at what brought David and Rachel, our *Chosson* and *Kallah,* successfully to the *chupah.*

After this couple had met, gone out and reached the predictable impasse, Rachel called to ask for assistance in deciding about her future with David. At first the dating seemed promising. But she needed to know and feel something "special", and it wasn't happening. Now they were at a standstill. Boredom and that old "lack of chemistry" feeling began to set in. She was confused, the clock was ticking. She wanted to marry and start a family, but she needed to know and feel more about him. "Was I wrong to ask about someone's life and feelings before I say I am ready to marry him?"

Over a two month period, Rachel and I secretly "conspired" together. She was courageous and took risks, blindly following my intuitive advice and guidance.

Together, we stumbled and discovered many of the lessons about creating a relationship through dating that you will read about in this book. Our phone consultations before and after dates were strategy sessions for opening gambits, personal questions and developing an inventory of responses to look for to indicate he was serious. After her dates, she would report on the time spent together. Every date was filled with ups and downs, surprise events, and moments of exhilaration. We chronicled each move, forward and backward, focusing on each nuance and measuring the mood, the temperature, the feeling. The more we measured, sometimes two or three times a day, the more we realized that something was happening. They were actually moving forward toward increasingly serious and emotionally fulfilling experiences. We learned that dating, when planned and carefully monitored, had an enormous potential to create environments of emotional honesty and depth. The prospect of marriage was becoming something tangible and real.

They developed their relationship moment by moment, date by date. Together they navigated each level, experiencing the security and trust required to feel that marriage is right. They opened the same pathways of togetherness that many of you will also experience. These were uncharted waters for them. For you, the course has already been marked, the mine fields cleared away.

IV. The Power of Dating

≋ The 3 Ns —
Now, Never Or Nurturance

For many mature singles, dating has become a painfully tedious and repetitious experience which should end before it begins. One reason is that they don't know what a reasonable time frame is to feel ready for marriage. "Shaya," I was recently asked. "do you believe in love at first sight?" The question has no answer. It seeks to validate a myth about entering into a trance of love at the first moment and never leaving it.

IV. THE POWER OF DATING

Love evolves over time as two people learn to overcome the challenges of building a life together. Love is a process of continually finding new resources within yourself for giving and nurturing another person.

Dating is the first environment between two people where they test their ability to nurture each other. When dating serves this purpose, it becomes an enormously exciting tool to create a relationship. On the other side of this nurturance, there are two polar opposites: "now" and "never." While they are opposites, they are also the same. Because both represent either the simplistic notion of "love at first sight," or the embittered entrapment of "love never happens." I compare "now" and "never" with a third "N" for nurturance.

≜ *Now*

Now is an attitude which says: "I want to go out today and fall in love. I want you to be in love with me today. And I want you to start off as my perfect ideal of my *bashert* and never change. All this has to happen today. Just show up and let's sign the contract!" This "Now" sense of relationships distorts how commitment and true intimacy grow. "Now" says "I'm already thirty-five, and I can't waste any time. If I see we're not compatible on the phone or after the first date, then I don't want to continue."

I vividly remember a "now" scene from many years ago in the 1960s. It was during the Vietnam and Hippie era. It seemed like it came right out of a Hollywood script. I walked into a shop in New York's Lower East Side and passed a couple who were talking to each other with an intensity reserved for the oldest and most intimate of friends. They looked like two lovers. The clothing and hair length was pure Haight Ashbury, East Village, anti war, pro peace and all the other icons of the Vietnam era. They walked into the shop after me, holding hands, and made a small purchase. The young woman turned to leave. They held hands for as long as possible, as if she was leaving him for a long period. There was a sense of sadness at the separation. She left the young man alone and very sad. The cashier, obviously intrigued by their intimacy, asked: "Where'd your girlfriend go?"

"I don't know, just somewhere."

"With a beautiful girlfriend like that and you don't know?"

"Hey, man," he says "she's not my girlfriend, we just met."

Here is a couple that fell in and out of love in moments. Almost like kittens playing with a ball of yarn, until the next toy of fascination strikes their fancy. The expectation that "now" love and trust can happen and ever amount to anything is a naïve dream of desperation frequently borne out of years of hurt and frustration.

Yes, there are couples who can date a relatively few times and decide to marry. They are usually younger couples, whose concept about relationships are still young and are under the influence of their parent's guidance and support. They are also living through a period of their lives when engagements and marriage are occurring with great frequency and regularity. Under these circumstances there is a desire to feel a part of the limelight and excitement. I have, *baruch Hashem* witnessed this phenomenon in my own home and in schools I've taught in. There is an electricity in the air.

But, the decision to marry is never easy. It requires support, guidance, love and an internal balance throughout the internal storms of two lives undergoing remarkable changes. A father of a young bride told me, "I knew she was serious when she came home after the third date and said she was too nervous to eat, or sleep, or do anything else. We didn't really know what to do for her. We just listened and tried to keep her on a steady course." Once this young girl gets older and is outside of the sphere of parental influence the calming effects are not as available.

Many mature singles who want to meet the *bashert* of their dreams "now," still harbor illusions of the quick fix date. Their inability to find that magic formula leads to continued disappointment and frustration. The problem is not them. There is no solid basis to their unrealistic expectations. What is closer to the reality? One's *bashert* is someone you grow together with over time. Relationships are carefully formed and develop only through great care, commitment, mutual nurturance and a readiness to change and grow. Everything else is illusion.

≋ Sometimes Feelings are too Intense

Another form of "now" is that some singles feel the need to share their intense feelings immediately. I find this to be true of many mental health professionals who have been taught to understand that the open expressions of feelings are at the heart of emotional health and enduring relationships. Much of psychotherapy is devoted to helping clients express their feelings. It makes sense for them to open their feelings early in a dating relationship and then expect the same from their date. Their message is: "I will share my feelings with you now, at this early stage of our relationship, because I want to show you that this is the kind of serious no nonsense relationship I want to have with my spouse. If you are as open as I am, then we have a future. If you are not, then I must go on to the next person."

I know of one man, a psychiatrist in his mid 40s, who dates continuously. His criteria for a wife is that, aside from all the other roles and tasks of a wife, she needs to recognize the importance of feelings. He tests this very early in their relationship. He called me one day last year to tell me of a wonderful date he had. He was sure this was the "right" person. He can't recall someone understanding him so well, someone so open and emotionally honest. But when he called back for a second date, she wasn't interested. He couldn't understand. He was so sure that they hit it off. How could she be so open and then say no? I tried to tell him that she was probably scared away. But he couldn't hear me. He clung to his need to express himself and discover the true person "now," at the beginning. He didn't understand that relationships have to build slowly before intense feelings can be shared. Feelings can only be bared as a relationship progresses.

⹋ *Never*

How many times have you heard the following: "I can't understand it. They were going out for so long. Everything seemed to be working between them. Then all of a sudden, when it came time to make the commitment, he (she) said; "I can't go through with it."

I heard of three separate situations like this in a matter of one week. In each situation, the couple had been seeing each other for months on end. Friends, family, everyone was certain, "This was it. *Baruch Hashem.*" But in all three situations, the same phenomenon occurred. Someone said: "It just didn't click for me. We were going out and going out. But I realized that we would never be happy. I'm doing it for both of us."

"Never" is the opposite of now. "Never" happens when a person continuously dates in an endless pursuit of that magical unmistakable certainty and experience. It's the epiphany which says: "Finally, this is the person I have been searching for. I don't have a shadow of doubt and have checked out every last detail and every last possibility. At last, the glass slipper finally fits!"

"Never" is based on that elusive moment of unquestioned certainty. It permits the players to continuously move the end zone further ahead. No matter how far you go up field, you never seem to score the touchdown. The problem is frequently that these players don't want to.

One young man shared his philosophy with me, clearly a rationalization of the "never" group. "You know, before you marry someone you want to make sure they can deal with a life crisis."

I asked him: "How long do you think it takes to see if someone can cope with crises?"

"It may take a couple of years." he answered.

Don't you somehow get the feeling that this young man may never walk down an aisle to his own *chupah*?

Let's be clear. Never is a function of avoidance and fear. Inside there are frightening thoughts of entrapment in a life of unhappiness and deprivation. There is the fear of losing what is most precious – the lifestyle of being a single that they have created.

⸙ *Nurturance*

The expectation for the instant intimacy of "now" is just as meaningless as "never." Both are mirror images of each other and non-starters, because they are based on unrealistic and infantile notions of how relationships develop, grow and eventually lead to marriage. For a relationship to grow there must be another dimension. This is not fueled by the need for instant feedback, like an instant lottery winner. Nor is it based on the absolute certainty we associate with Federally insured savings. This dimension is focused not on time, but on giving to create a relationship. Therefore, the 3rd N is for nurturance. Nurturance is at the heart of all meaningful relationships between a husband and wife and the glue which bonds all people emotionally. The only true qualities which make a difference in dating which leads to marriage are acts of *chesed*. Caring and understanding are at the heart of this nurturance. And this relationship based on *chesed* and nurturance is consistent throughout married life.

IV. THE POWER OF DATING

🕯 *A Chassdic Tale About Nurturance*

This point is at the heart of a *chassidic* tale which I have found very helpful as a way of describing the essence of nurturance between a husband and wife- in this case two dating partners:

An aged *tzaddik* was nearing the end of his years. While he had lived a life of purity, kindness and complete honesty, he still needed that last hint of reassurance that his life was well lived. He prayed to *Hashem* to be shown the difference between *Gan Eden*, where he would be going and its counterpart, *Gehennom*, reserved for those whose lives were spent in dishonesty and destructiveness. His request was granted. An emissary was sent to escort him through the two worlds.

They arrived at the nether world. He expected to see fire and brimstone. Instead he saw a pastoral setting. At the far end of a field there stood a cottage. He and his escort entered. Seated around a table were emaciated bodies, groaning in their hunger. Placed at the center of the table was a large bowl of stew with a wondrous aroma.

"Why can't they eat?" asked the *tzaddik*,

"Because they have no elbow bones and can't bend their elbows to place the food in their mouths."

The *tzaddik* was shaken and upset at the sight of starvation and asked to move on. He understood that in their lives they had never fed others and now they were consigned to an afterlife of starvation.

They arrived at the world of *Gan Eden*. From the outside it looked like the other world, complete with the same cottage at the end of the field. They entered and saw the same table and the same stew. But the faces were cherubic and filled with life. The *tzaddik* said: "Here their reward is that they have elbows."

"No," said the escort. "Here they also have no elbow bones. But here, they feed each other."

The ability to give is the difference between people who are starving and those who feel sated. Nurturing moments are the basis of a relationship which can lead to marriage. Every act of giving must be followed by another. Each level of growth requires a new stage of commitment. The notion that love "happens" is reflective of an immature understanding of the nature of a close, lasting relationship. Love is created through nurturance.

⚜ *To Make a Difference, Someone Has To Be In Charge*

Relationships go by the wayside because they are controlled by people who either want now or never. To make a difference someone has to know where things are headed. Someone responsible for making things happen has to be in charge. I was shocked to hear someone tell me that a national Frum dating service gets eighty to ninety couples a week together. The number of couples who develop serious relationships with each other is negligible. Mature singles frequently view initial dates as a breaking in period, just to "get comfortable." The reality is that they have no choice because they just don't know how to get serious. The result is wasted opportunities. No one is in control of the process. They don't know where they are going because they have never been through the journey before. They don't

IV. THE POWER OF DATING

know the territory and don't have a map or a guide. Nothing moves, chaos prevails and innocent and precious people get hurt.

When I was first training as a therapist I had a rather blunt and in-your-face supervisor. After finishing an interview with a couple who literally walked all over me, she looked at me over her glasses and in the most condescending fashion said: "Shaya, in a professional relationship there is usually a therapist and a client in a room together. It is preferable that you know who is who."

I got the chills and also got the message right between the eyes and never forgot it. When two or more people are striving to achieve something, someone has to know where they are going, or else no one gets anywhere.

One of the best stories I have ever heard which demonstrates this issue of benevolent and productive control is one I have used with many married couples over the years:

A young man was close to a great and very important *rosh yeshivah* who devoted himself completely to the needs of others. The young man watched over him and made sure his needs were met. The *rosh yeshivah* was well into his seventies and somewhat frail.

One evening the young man accompanied the *rosh yeshivah* home after a long and tiring day. When they arrived, the *rebbetzin* showed her husband where his dinner was waiting for him. Just as the *rosh yeshivah* sat down the phone rang. The *rebbetzin* made a signal not to take it because he was quite tired. However, he took the call and spent a few minutes discussing a *sholom bayis* issue with a distraught woman. The *rebbetzin* was quite upset out of concern for her husband's health. The *rosh yeshivah* finished with the call and returned to his waiting meal. Later, when the student was alone with the *rosh yeshivah* he asked: "I can't understand why you helped someone else with a *sholom bayis* issue while you created one in your own home." The *rosh yeshivah* answered very patiently. He said: "There was no *sholom bayis* issue in my house, only in the other one. With the woman who called there were two people fighting, here there was only one."

The *rosh yeshivah* was saying that when someone is in charge, interactions are productive and don't get out of hand. It's the same with dating. If you can read the map and understand just how to shepherd this relationship, then your chances of marriage increase exponentially. This program will teach you how to take control and guide a relationship on through marriage.

☙ *The Lost Focus*

Without this control, dating continuously fails to deliver any measurable results. So, strategies must be employed to maintain a viable and productive social lifestyle. Social calendars are filled with workshops, Shabbatonim, lectures and singles mixers. For the more determined, psychotherapists are turned to in an attempt to facilitate marriage through personal insight.

Then there are professional "singles marketers," many of whom have discovered a thriving and lucrative business through the promise of offering "hope" through a never-ending chain of "singles events." The results of these events are best experienced in the profits they generate for their promoters. There are also events planned from the *chesed* side. These are run by dedicated volunteers who have devoted sleepless nights to arranging Shidduchim and gatherings. Yet, as one such volunteer recently told me: "I work day and night. I get them together. But nothing happens."

No matter how we get singles together, they must never be left to negotiate the minute by minute process of the date by themselves. For dates to pay off, they must be planned, reviewed, assessed and most important of all, follow a tried and true formula that works over a reasonable span of time. Only through a clear overview of what makes a relationship work, stage by stage, and careful attention to the minutest detail of human interaction can singles create emotionally meaningful experiences leading directly to marriage.

Mature singles need to be trained, and guided. Nothing can be left to chance. The next time you walk into a bank and have to patiently wait as a supervisor watches over a teller trainee until he gets it right, remember that this trainee is being taught in a way that makes a difference. Singles must negotiate *krias yam soof* alone. They are brought together and then told to swim across themselves.

It's the date that matters most and there is no way of comparing the personal reflections shared in the therapists office, or skills learned in an experiential workshop against the actual "real time" of the dating experience. It's similar to the difference between trying to teach swimming on a carpet as opposed to teaching swimming in a pool. It's a whole different world when you hit the water. On a date, when you are emotionally prepared, when you have a road map in front of you and maintain the focus and know what you're trying to achieve, then you're in control and this makes all the difference. I found that when these elements were in place relationships began to blossom and unfold. I began to understand that dating has the power to transform lives.

I recently spoke to Harold, a thirty-seven year old teacher who dated a young woman for the first time. He had attended a workshop I had recently given and had the chance to put the theory to use. He followed the script and prepared his material. He knew what he was looking for. When he finished the date, he called me. He was both elated and overwhelmed. I asked him why. He said that the elation was because for the first time he knew where he was headed on a date. He had a focus and a mission. He was overwhelmed because after years of going out something very real and personal had occurred between him and another person. I had another thought I wanted to tell him, but held back. This was that when one is emotionally moved, there is frequently a feeling of vulnerability. Suddenly one cares and it's hard to protect oneself in the real world of relationships. I held back from telling him everything. After all, it was still his first date.

≑ *Opening The World of Emotions & Closeness*

This program is based on connecting the inner lives of two people and releasing a world of emotional energy between them through the dating experience. It succeeds by taking issues which are at the heart of our lives and saying: "This is what I think is important to talk about because it's at the center my consciousness and life." The content of what is shared must be a part of a progressive emotional march forward. With each date appropriate levels of the attachment grow, progressively and poignantly.

Marriage depends on human closeness. Shared emotions of caring and concern are the glue to all human relationships. This is how *Hashem* created us. These feelings are the basis of our prayers, our expressions of love, gratitude and caring for each other. In this same way they are the human bonding material between husband and wife. We learn in *Beraishes* how *Rivka Imainu* stumbled off her camel when she saw *Yitzchok Avenu* for the first time. The Torah may be telling us about a young woman being overwhelmed by emotions when seeing a man for the first time who may very well be her partner for life. And *Yitzchok Avenu* is overcome by similar emotions when he takes her to his mother's tent and for the first time since his mother's death he begins to feel comforted. The Torah understands our needs for closeness and emotional intimacy as the fabric of marriage.

Feelings between two people who are dating are as complex and deep as our *neshomos*. They reflect the deepest aspects of our souls. The primary purpose of dating is to learn how to experience these feelings with another person and reach a certainty that the relationship will endure for a lifetime as husband and wife.

≋ A Generation Which Has Lost Emotions

Today we live in a world where it's difficult to understand what emotions really are. Our deeper human feelings have been corrupted by a society driven by technology, consumerism and a massive media net. Sooner or later the impact of this society touches everyone living in it.

For so many Jewish singles, as in the rest of Jewish society in America, we can apply the old Yiddish expression *"Vie es kristel zich, yiddelt zich."* The way a Christian society moves, so do we, as Jews, move in similar ways. It requires a superhuman effort to build a barrier between our world and the culture around us. Very few succeed. This is certainly true of the world of emotions. What are emotions in 1999 America? Emotions are no longer shared human experiences which bind two people for life. In America, emotions are primarily media driven. They are seasonal. I was recently asked on a radio program what I thought about Valentine's Day. My response was that on this day Hallmark sells more cards than for any other single day of the year. This is how the emotions of Americans are constantly manipulated to drive an economy.

Consider how an entire nation waited and watched and cried tears of pride and joy as a huge amiable and muscular baseball player, Mark McGuire, hit home run after home run. He hit his sixty-second home run and waved at his father sitting in the stands celebrating his sixty-second birthday. A nation was deeply "moved" as he rounded the bases. He picked up his young son as he crossed home plate and we were even more touched. America's media caters to the human need for "meaningful and touching moments." We call it entertainment. It touches us, just as it touches the non-Jewish and non-Torah world, and corrupts our sense of what human relationships really are. The Superbowl, the World series, the Oscar Awards all manipulated our emotions like the keys of a piano. We are played deftly and expertly by the marketing and media geniuses who drive this culture. As a result most of us are confused and no longer know what true emotions are.

Which emotions have the power to bind two people together as husband and wife? How do we define them? How do we structure experiences which enable two people to experience magical and meaningful moments with each other? How do we bring two frequently hurt and vulnerable people out of their emotional closet and offer them the opportunity to be moved to the point of actually caring enough to make a lifetime commitment to each other?

These questions are the essence of our challenge and are the springboard for our approach. Older singles are not unlike the rest of society. They have found it wiser and more prudent not to expose their emotions on dates. For some, feelings are a strange and dangerous alien world. After years of dating, it's too difficult to feel still any emotional responses. I'll call it burnout.

As professionally successful people, many Jewish singles are physicians, financial analysts, lawyers and mental health professionals. These professional roles are all consuming, providing tons of gratification, requiring unfailing commitment and leaving everyone thoroughly drained. Is there any room left for emotions?

Under these conditions emotions become buried, or distorted by media driven images of "falling in love." When two people are together, each waiting for some special sign or event to occur, a vacuum is created. This vacuum is quickly filled with doubt, disappointment and distance. With true feelings playing a back seat to media, fear of exposure and professional burn out, there is little chance that many singles can reach that required stage of certainty and caring for each other. The result is that many singles feel an ongoing sense of profound emptiness in their relationships with their dates. Yes, there is a deep desire to find their *bashert*. Yet, they just can't achieve the state of emotional connection they need to consider marriage.

☙ *Shop Till You Drop*

Before I discuss the emotions which are the power source for our program, permit me to digress for a moment and describe my experience as a marketing consultant for a shopping mall.

I was once consulting for a shopping mall developer creating a "greeters" program. Greeters stand by the mall entrance, smile and say : "Hi, welcome to the Enterprise Mall." When shoppers enter the mall they are frequently confused and overwhelmed. So greeters are the first person shoppers meet. Their impact is to calm down and orient shoppers so that they buy more and return to the mall. We discovered an interesting phenomenon. If the greeter wore a suit from Donna Karan or an outfit from the Gap, then sales for that store skyrocketed. The reason was quite simple. When a person goes shopping, they have invested thousands of hours in advertising and marketing which has led them to this mall to make their purchase. You don't have to create the desire to buy, it's already there, courtesy of NBC, CBS and all the other media networks which have primed them for this great moment of shopping. They hit the mall like a desert nomad hits an oasis. The greeter doesn't have to say a word, she merely wears merchandise. The shopper sees the merchandise and "boom," the connection is made. So Donna Karan sales shoot up 100% for any week the greeter wears her line. The waiting list of merchandisers who wanted greeters to wear their outfits is two months long.

☙ *Drama Under A Calm Facade*

The same dynamics of accumulated emotions are at work with singles. Each single approaches a date with countless hopes, wishes, fears, dreams and fantasies. His or her one primary life goal is marriage. Each single, like the mall shopper without the greeter, becomes overwhelmed and disoriented by a myriad of conflicting feelings they harbor. The result is a tightening up in a defensive mode. Nothing can be shown or revealed.

Watch couples dating in the lobbies of hotels, walking together through a botanical garden, sharing a meal together with practiced and distant etiquette. They converse quietly and politely. On the surface all appears to be quiet and under control. Under the surface however, there is the commotion of their emotional lives.

Still waters run deep. Under the surface, emotions are present in their most intricate and sensitive expressions. Here and there they manage to emerge- through dreams, through tears shed at a personal *simcha* or through thoughts about a clock ticking silently away. Many singles may not even make the connection between feelings experienced in one setting, like visiting a family on Shabbos, and the desire to find that one special person. Beneath the calm surface there is a very powerful drama being played out in silence, beyond awareness.

≉ *Defining The Inner Drama*

What is this inner drama? It's the inner fantasies, visions, hopes and dreams of marriage which have been fermenting deep inside since childhood. The promise of marriage once lived very vividly in the heart of all singles. It is our gift and promise from *Hashem*. On the surface it may be lost, but underneath it lives on.

I remember quite vividly working with a young boy whose father had suddenly and tragically passed away after a brief and unexpected illness. There was no time for him to emotionally prepare for the tragedy or say goodbye. He was in shock and was now having a hard time adjusting in school. I tried to discuss the loss with him. He told me that "he felt nothing and didn't even care." I was persistent and asked him if he ever dreamed. "Sometimes," he said. He came back to me a while later, somewhat sheepish and wanting to talk. He remembered that he did have a dream immediately after his father's sudden death: "You were right. I did have a dream. I was walking toward this corner and I felt him coming toward me from around the other corner. My heart was pounding real hard, like it was going to break. Even though I couldn't see him, I could feel him coming closer. Any second and we would both reach the corner together and see each other and be together once again. And my heart was beating louder and louder."

His heart was dictating his dreams. You can't suppress love and loss without it bobbing to the surface like a float. It has a life of its own. When I think of singles who have extinguished the fire in their hearts and minds and tell me they feel very little, I invariably think of this young boy and I wait for them to dream to realize the feelings of loss driving the dream.

Losing a father is a tragedy of terrible proportions. But losing the hope and dream of marriage, the promise of love, family and children is also a tragedy. Perhaps even greater. Losing a father is losing one person, losing the dream of marriage means losing many lives, losing a future. Somewhere, somehow the heart still carries with it expectations which run deep and to the very marrow and core of existence. I always trust that the heart fights the ominous threat of a life consigned to loneliness. Not loneliness from friends or a community of peers. But loneliness for that one special intimate relationship with whom life is dedicated and shared and with whom one builds and creates new lives.

In dating, regardless of the denials, I know all singles have a secret wish to remedy this loneliness. Please, don't make the mistake of believing that profoundly deep feelings are not there with each date. They are there, with each and every date. This program uses dates in a focused and disciplined manner. In each individual is an immense power from the dreams that live inside everyone. The drama is the emotions of *Hashem's* creations, crying out for their lost partner in life. This is what must be worked with on each date — to bring these feelings to the surface in a disciplined and appropriate way. You learn to communicate through these feelings, your jewels, and wait for them to create a ripple on the surface of the person you are dating. We decipher these hidden feelings coming to the surface on the "royal pond" and learn how to move the relationship forward.

Accept this principle as an article of faith: when two people are dating, yourselves or others, and are quietly and calmly communicating with each other, perhaps over a glass of Coke in a hotel lobby, or walking down a shaded path through a garden, there is a drama being played out underneath the spoken words. Beneath the quiet and reserved veneer, there is enough energy in motion to redirect lives. Together they posses a combined energy strong enough to transform their lives. The challenge is that neither one knows how to start off this chain of events to utilize the ocean of emotional energy living beneath the surface.

≈ *Creating Moments Of Meaning*

The goal of this program is to effectively utilize the precious ore of emotions which each of you carries within yourselves. You will learn how to recognize and then share these feelings in a safe, gradual and progressive manner, step by step. First, slowly creating something precious between yourself and your dating partner. Too slow, and the relationship withers. Too fast, and it frightens. Using the seven gate principal, at least one of you and at times, both of you, observe the subtle and gentle ripples on the surface of the pond. Each ripple represents the emergence of this inner emotional life. The cumulative results of these moments of meaningful connection are the creation of a relationship which leads gradually yet surely to an ultimate personal commitment between two people — marriage. No moment is wasted. No opportunity is missed in determining whether you are indeed closer to the prize of your life-long search.

≋ *The Prism*

How do we effectively release and use this energy? Consider the analogy of a prism used to break up light waves. Just as a prism takes in white light and separates it into many colors in an orderly fashion, our seven gates of a relationship provide clear and progressive expression for the emotional life residing within you. Feelings of such force need to be broken down into manageable experiences. Each jewel represents a precise emotional connection specific to the stage of your development in dating. When you communicate with each other in a focused and intentional way at any given stage, you are casting a jewel on to the pond and creating an energized arc of emotional vitality specific to a stage between two people. When you are focusing on affirmations, jewels of communication are cast into the relationship. You then await the ripples.

Emotions and experiences between you are very specific to a given stage and are evaluated only in respect to this area. They are not tumultuous roller coaster experiences muddled by 1001 conflicting feelings and facts. There is a clarity and a way of evaluating the level of the relationship and its growth. Moments are grounded in precious and subtle human connections. Each of the seven gates becomes the clear and progressive articulation of your deepest feelings about love, marriage, trust, commitment and family. The gates lead to a transformation, from two people leading separate and independent lives, to two people sharing an emotional bond of caring and commitment for each other.

These are the value-laden underpinnings of the relationship you will attempt to create during dating. The rest of this book is dedicated solely to a practical guide of "how to":

- *develop your Inner Circle*
- *develop a clear focus on hope and belief*
- *find your precious jewels and cast them into the pond of your relationship*
- *learn to decipher the beautiful song and story of the ripples you have created*
- *move through the 7 gates to marriage.*

V. Beginning the Journey

⚘ Crossing A Rushing Stream

Throughout the writing of this book I was continuously brought back to a memory of a hike in the early spring. The hiking trail took us through the woods, showing the first signs of spring, warmer weather, and blossoms promising to follow. There were also still signs of winter. As we got deeper into the woods, the trail became icy and slippery. The path through the woods led us to a swift rushing stream. We wanted to continue, but hesitated. No one was sure enough to cross. Somewhere, crossing the stream, we knew there was a path of smooth rocks which would get us across because, from a distance, we had seen others cross it. But when we approached the stream and looked for the rocks, the murky rushing waters covered our path across. To cross the stream we needed someone to guide us from one rock to the next. One wrong step and we would be left with soaking and very cold feet ...

The road to marriage is similar to crossing a stream with its path submerged and obscured by rushing waters. You have to know where the stones are, get your feet firmly planted on the right first one and then move on to the next, until you're on the other side. Dating is a progressive relationship toward marriage. You have to know where to step, be very steady and have great balance. There are limitless wrong moves and very few right steps across the stream. The right ones bring you across, safe and dry. The wrong steps lead to icy waters.

Some singles, after too many missed attempts, feel there is no way of knowing how to make it across. They go through the motions of dating, but inside lies a gnawing feeling that they will never reverse a life of being alone. They continue to date, taking their first tenuous steps into the stream, but inside, can't see themselves making it across.

What happens? They put their foot on the first rock protruding from the water. They call, go on a first date, perhaps even a second. Then they can't go any further. There is an uncertainty about what to say or do. They've become frozen in superficial exchanges. If you ask one or both why it never went any further, you might hear that there were "no feelings between us" or there was a "lack of chemistry."

I had been called by an engineer, Saul, who was dating a young woman named Ellen. Both were in their 30s. He felt stuck, and uncertain as to whether he wanted to continue. After we spoke he realized he really did want to continue to see her. He called to make another date. They went out again and she told him she was not interested in continuing. I spoke to Ellen myself. She told me, "We went out for three months and I was waiting for him to get serious. He never did. I got hurt and decided to end it. Now that he's decided to continue, I can't feel for him again so easily. For now, I have to say I can't continue."

Saul was unable to move off the first rock. He could only be sociable. That was it. There was no way for him to move the relationship on to a more mature and serious level.

For others, it's just the opposite. Each new relationship begins with great anticipation and excitement. They have the ability to see new relationships as holding the promise of marriage. There is an earnest commitment to make sure that the next person will be their *bashert*. They start with drive and determination, ready to race head first across the stream. They're filled with *bitochon* that this time they'll succeed. They step on the first rock, jump to the second and even the third. But, somehow, as the relationship intensifies, they are overcome by doubts about going out too far into the stream. They start to see flaws, problems, questions about their "compatibility." They feel they went out too far, too fast. They reconsider. That's when you hear the line: "It's a good thing I thought about the relationship more seriously. I almost reached a point of no return." Now, once again, they are alone.

There is still another group who try to avoid the stream completely. They have decided to wait for winter to move on, the waters to clear and for the ice to give way to the spring thaw before they venture across the stream. They want to see "exactly where they are going." They wait and wait. But the water always remains murky and spring never arrives. All these singles face the same challenge. They do not know how to get across. They have no clue as to how to get through a dating relationship.

Dating should be a means to progressively build a relationship, step by step, carefully measuring commitment, closeness, openness and caring. I have developed seven distinct phases to the dating process. Each must be developed and solidified before entering the next. Each phase may take a day, week or month. It depends on how you integrate new experiences. Each level provides you with a discussion of a concept, anecdotes, examples, a visualization or a fantasy to give you a personal and up-close feeling, as well as interpersonal exercises to help you build your emotional muscles. The entire program is framed by two central concepts. The first is called Jewels in the Pond and the second is your Inner Circle.

☙ Casting Jewels Into The Pond

It's 6:15 AM. You get out of bed, hit the light, turn on the water, perk the coffee, make a call, hit the elevator button, etc. Later in the day you call on a client, make a pitch and wait to see if you made the sale. Since waking up you have initiated many operations. With each action you touched or did something and waited; for the light, the water, the elevator, or the client to respond to something you initiated. That night you go on a date and you are clueless as to how to make something happen. You wait. In the end, nothing happens and you go home.

V. Beginning The Journey

Some areas of life are very precise and quite demanding about behavior and expectations. Other areas are less precise. Dating should be one of those areas where you initiate events, know what you're looking for and wait for a response. To make things happen you have to be precise and very observant. Your carefully worded messages and well thought out questions are like casting "jewels into the pond." When you drop them into the "pond" of the relationship you should know what you are looking for. Observe the ripples as you communicate with the person you are dating in a very personal and meaningful way. Observe and consider whether the relationship is growing in each of the seven gates.

Joy called me after her 3rd date with Allen. The first two were fine. We had gone over her strategy for the 3rd date. She used it just as we had planned. Allen was stone faced. There was no response on the "pond." She started to feel it was all over. Then she said to herself, "I have to try again until I get a response one way or the other." She said "Allen, I just told you something which I thought would have meaning to you and you didn't respond. Does it mean that you don't care?" Allen's face turned sad. He was at a loss to respond and said so. She asked if she could help him. By the end of the date there was a clear desire for both to continue. Joy had learned to expect a response. When she didn't get one, she went after it another way.

Regardless of who you are, your age, or your previous dating experiences, every single has the ability to create these ripples, to open up relationships and discover the right person to marry. The issue is not "is there anyone out there for me." As my wife's high school teacher told her more than a few years ago: "For every pot there's a cover." It's a matter of teaching you how to cast your jewels and understand the ripples they have created. This becomes your key in recognizing your *bashert*.

≑ A Visualization: Jewels Cast On The Royal Pond

To better help you understand and internalize the meaning of the jewels and the ripples they create, here is a visualization or a fantasy to try. Like all the other visualizations in this book, use these steps to get a deeper sense of the experience we are trying to create for you.

1. *Find a quiet place.*
2. *Read the visualization over once and become acquainted with the concepts.*
3. *Repeat the visualization with your eyes closed.*

Imagine yourself on a lovely bridge in a Japanese garden. The waters beneath the bridge are still and serene, reflecting pink blossoms on the dark liquid mirror. You can smell the aroma of the blossoms. In your hand you have a wine colored velvet pouch containing seven small jewels, each the size of a barley grain.

You remove a jewel from the pouch and gently let it drop into the pond beneath you. You watch as the jewel touches the water. As it gently touches the water, you watch the subtle ringlets form in concentric circles around the disappearing jewel. You can see the undulating ripples gently forming and moving outward, like soft waves. Now you can even feel the gentle ripples moving within yourself. They are calming and relaxing.

When you are searching for your *bashert* and you ask a question, or make a statement about your relationship, the process is as subtle as these gentle ripples, as faint as a whisper. You gently cast your jewel to understand whether you and this person are on the same journey in life, speak the same emotional language, have the potential to share a life together. Through a series of these jewels tossed into the delicate pond of the relationship, a bond is given a chance to grow and blossom. Each stage of the relationship requires its own jewels and creates it distinctive ripples.

Now that this concept has been introduced, we can proceed to the central concept in this book, your Inner Circle.

VI. Introduction to Your Inner Circle

☙ *Learning To Be The Real You*

*I*n the numerous workshops I've given to singles, I've come to face probably the most difficult of all challenges facing singles. The strength to marry requires the deepest of all human relationships. The bond between a parent and child may be deeper. But, this relationship doesn't require any effort. It is biological. This is who you are, like it or not. Marriage requires the creation of affection, trust, love, security, support, esteem and countless other feelings which touch the heart. The challenge is simply that so many singles have no clue as to how to build a relationship based on these feelings. The prevailing climate of dates is so frequently characterized by emotional distance, defensiveness, and unrealistic hopes which all lead to disappointment.

VI. Introduction To Your Inner Circle

When I first began working with mature singles, I misread the problem. I interpreted their continued failures as self inflicted. A couple of years ago, when I began presenting workshops, I met Avi. He was in his late 40s. On the outside he was self sufficient and very orderly in his life as a single man. On the inside he was painfully lonely. He managed to earn a livable wage as a bookkeeper and tried to appear well groomed, but fell short of a polished appearance. He reminded me of a blind person who dressed himself without anyone around to straighten his tie. Nothing hung right. Yet, despite what I saw as areas which required some work before he could attract a wife, Avi insisted that he intended to marry a woman who was pretty, shared his *hashkofos* and insisted that she be no older than her mid to upper 30s. Obviously, he had plans for a growing family. But, he was patient. He would "wait it out" until his criteria were met.

I was filled with a mixture of sadness and anger at hearing his checklist. Here he was alone and lonely, his clock was ticking away. Soon he would hit 50. He had very little to offer. Yet he was making all the demands. I saw a man destined to be alone for the rest of his life.

I could understand that even someone who is not earning a great salary and lacks sophistication in his dress and appearance could attract a woman if he has the emotional depth. But, Avi was just as ill suited in this area as in the others. When I looked closer I understood that emotional development and expressiveness, which is the key to developing a relationship which can lead to marriage, was more problematic than all the other areas between single men and women. Women have a greater intuitive sense of emotional closeness and feelings. Men are more distant, and have a more difficult time with feelings.

As I started to work with other singles, I observed many variations of "Avi." Some were men, others were women. All shared a single underlying difficulty: their inability to create and sustain a deep relationship led to an inability to appropriately judge who could be *bashert*. And without being connected to your deepest self you cannot recognize your *bashert*. Imagine two people making up to meet at Grand Central Station at 5:00 PM. They spend quite a bit of time talking on the phone and developed in their mind's eye an image of what the other looks like. What they fail to do is corroborate these inner images of the other and fail to identify their distinguishing characteristics. Both will wait until the last train leaves, each thinking he or she was stood up. They may have both been standing side by side, even bumping into each other, while waiting. Each was relying on an unrealistic internal image that could not guide them in a real relationship.

Dating couples share Cokes, pleasant small talk, a great meal, concert or a stroll in a magnificent garden. None of these life's pleasures will help either of them recognize that the other is their *bashert*. This is only experienced by an inner core of emotional clarity which enables you to "see" the deeper side of another person and provides an ability to show and feel closeness, emotional warmth and caring — the qualities for creating an emotional bond necessary for marriage. Even if there were a desire to be expressive and share this deeply personal side, which could be understood and appreciated, the territory is usually too strange and frightening.

VI. Introduction To Your Inner Circle

I consistently met other "Avis," who never learned that at the heart of marriage lies the necessity to be emotionally warm and giving. Without this ability and readiness, many singles resort to unrealistic standards which can never be met. They are lonely and disappointed. Gradually, I realized that the success of any program to help singles marry meant teaching emotionally guarded single men and women that under the surface of cautious and defensive social interaction can be a warm and caring heart. Without the ability for two people to emotionally talk to each other, nothing has any meaning in a relationship.

I began to search through my own experiences to discover a solution to the challenge of bringing together two individuals who are emotionally uncomfortable with each other. I was repeatedly drawn back to memories and feelings of caring individuals in my own life, some of whom are still alive and others who have passed on. In my memories I recalled precious moments of inspiration, closeness and trust. I spent many months carefully analyzing what I had received from each of these people over the years — my late father and grandparents, rebbeim, teachers, close friends. With each individual, I recalled the feelings related to their precious gifts of understanding, caring and concern for my development and well being. The more I began to understand their gifts and the warm and positive feelings they created within me, the more I was able to understand what enabled me to give to others in my profession as a family and marital therapist, as well as in my own life as a husband and father. These memories evoked a genuinely warm, giving and deeply human side of my personality. I could even use these memories in my *tefillos* to attain a sense of greater *kavannah* and deeper understanding of the meaning of my *tefillos*.

I realized that this inner side of myself, connected to a few precious relationships and memories of their gifts to me, was a prevalent reality in every person. The feelings and memories may get buried and forgotten, but they always remain deep inside. More important, this was the side of "Avi" that could develop a relationship with a woman. If Avi could have access to these feelings, he could use them to create a deep and meaningful relationship with a woman, who would sense that despite his disheveled appearance, he has the ability to be a husband. Appearances can be modified with just a bit of education. This wouldn't scare off a woman if she sensed there was something more profound beating inside him. I also sensed that with the return to one's deeper side, the absurd demands and unrealistic fantasies give way to sincere and meaningful feelings shared between two people.

For me, the Inner Circle has always played a very conscious role. As my father passed away when I was 10, I can vividly recall soaking up the influences of many people I learned to admire. I remember how, at the age of 22, while living in NY, I was suddenly gripped by the fear that my grandfather, living in Boston, was getting older and more frail. I needed to see him one more time to ask questions, feel his influence, hear his voice and understand whatever I could of him. That day I traveled to Boston and spent the next few days drinking in all I could. Within a few months he was gone.

To this day, over 30 years later I can still feel and

recount those precious moments. To this day, I can close my eyes and use those feelings to evoke a sense of trust and depth in myself as I travel through life. He is just one among many such people who inhabit my Inner Circle. I have come to learn that the mere memory or impression of such a person anchors me in a delicate and sensitive state of my own best feeling and visceral qualities. It enables me to reach out beyond myself and give to others. This is what is needed in the search for a life partner. Our Inner Circle creates a level of emotional honesty, chesed and true warmth which then becomes a series of building blocks in any meaningful relationship.

≅ *Your Inner Anchors*

I have always called this group of special people, who provided me with special chesed as my "Inner Circle." They are the foundation of my efforts. Our Inner Circle serves as an anchor to our inner voice, continuously guiding us to give, just as we have received emotional gifts from our own Inner Circle. This is the first element in developing a relationship worthy of marriage. In marriage you have to give, share and understand. You must continuously reach beyond yourself, take greater risks and relate to deeper feelings, more so than in any other relationship in your entire life.

As in my fable, the Inner Circle provides a guiding force within. That's why I have placed it at the heart of this program. As you proceed through each of the seven gates you are guided and strengthened by your own Inner Circle, to go beyond what you believed to be your emotional limits. Everything you say and do, which brings you closer to marriage, draws on this vast reservoir of understanding waiting quietly within you to find its true expression in life.

Recently I spoke to an older single who suffered because others could not see and feel he was a caring and loving person. On the surface he was highly intellectual, cold and distant. I understood why women would feel the need to distance themselves from him. I asked him who were the people to whom he felt closest to. He named a number of people who I happened to know. They were warm and caring and giving people. I told him that the same part of himself, which felt close to those who have given him so much in life, was the part of his personality needed to create a caring and loving relationship with a woman. He has the raw materials. He has to learn how use them. As you cultivate those deeper feelings associated with your Inner Circle, you will find an increasing capacity to create and hold on to special relationships.

≋ *A Concept From Beraishis*

The Inner Circle is not a new concept, but rather, my own crude way of paraphrasing the Torah's concept of *demus d'yokno*. This is an inner perception of someone's likeness. It is feeling the presence and influence of a beloved figure in your life. Rashi, the great commentator on the Torah, describes this in *Beraishis*, when *Yosef Hatzaddik* is in the grasp of the wife of Potiphar, the Egyptian Minister. He is a mere seventeen, exposed to a

VI. Introduction To Your Inner Circle

woman of power attempting to seduce him. The cumulative effects of the corrupt influences of Egypt have begun to reach him. Left to his own young and frail human resources, signs of moral weakening begin to emerge.

At that critical moment, when the fate of an entire people rests on the moral strength of an adolescent, he sees the likeness of his father, *Yaakov Avenu*. This is the *demus d'yokno*. With this inner image, he experiences the evocation of his own holiness- Kedusha- and his moral legacy as a Jew. He remembers that he is a child from the house of his grandfather, *Avrohom Avenu*. He finds the moral spark within himself to resist, back away and escape. And with this action of moral strength, his people can enter Egypt and emerge a nation to receive the Torah.

The Talmud later informs us that Yosef's moral strength goes on to serve as the power which enables the sea to split and for the redemption to be completed. For *Hashem* tells the sea, "Just as Yosef conquered his nature to resist Potiphar's wife, you too can conquer your nature and split to save *Am Yisroel*." Yosef was inspired by an inner image of greatness. This was the strength behind his moral greatness. This is what I mean by the Inner Circle. It's a part of each of us.

My brother-in-law, Rabbi Shmuel Kaufman, is one of the great *mechanchim* (Yeshivah educators) and *kiruv* (outreach) personalities born and raised in America. Recently, I heard him say to a friend: "Do you know why you're such an *erliche* (special) Yid? Because you were *zoche* (privileged) to see Reb Moshe (Feinstein). Just being next to him all those years made you who you are." Rabbi Feinstein, who died in 1984, was a man venerated by Jews throughout the globe and acknowledged to be one of the true Torah giants of the generation

He was telling this person that by being exposed to Reb Moshe and looking at his face, seeing him daven, watching him as he lived from day to day, he now had internalized his qualities. My brother-in-law was saying that Reb Moshe is now part of his friend's Inner Circle.

There are times when we can hear the voice, see the face, sense a guiding hand. Sometimes it's nebulous: a dream, a vague memory, or a nostalgic mood reminiscent of someone who had a deep impact on our lives and perception of the world. Each of us carries personalities and memories within ourselves. My program is built on helping you gain access to these powerful influences in your own life, and utilizing them in your search for your *bashert*.

☙ *Your Own Inner Circle*

Who are the voices and personalities who inspire you from within? These living influences of great hearts and souls who gave you so much of themselves as an expression of their towering spirits. These influences form our Inner Circle. They can be relationships with parents, grandparents, teacher, rabbis, friends and so many others. They can be alive or may have passed on. The essence they leave within us are moments of exquisite clarity related to feelings of trust, closeness and emotional security. We permitted ourselves to love these people because they left us with a feeling of caring and acceptance. Their gifts created an internal guiding force as natural as breathing, always there to influence and be

VI. Introduction To Your Inner Circle

heard by the attentive and sensitive listener attuned to the feeling, the voice and the message.

Living memories tell us that just as we felt close to these people of our Inner Circle, we can have deep and very meaningful relationships with other people for whom we care and who care for us. Frequently, at workshops, I have participants go through an exercise similar to the one at the end of this chapter. At first, there is skepticism about the ability to remember and feel these people from the Inner Circle and the memories associated with them. However, the great majority of participants find it easy and fascinating to evoke these memories. At times there is someone feeling depressed and hopeless, experiencing the scars of battle and defeat as a mature single. They doubt that they have an Inner Circle. I know differently.

Everyone has these special relationships living within. Otherwise they would be hollow and broken to the point of being unable to function. What they are expressing is a deep sense of sadness and loneliness which has, for the moment, obliterated the memories which mean so much to them. They were in fact given many gifts. For now, in their state of hurt and deprivation, they just can't remember. My approach is always the same. I say: "I know you were given many gifts by people who were and still are important to you.

If you permit yourself to remember the people you feel close to, you'll recall some very precious feelings and moments." I did this with a young man, Yoni, who attended the seminar. He was insistent that he had no memories nor an Inner Circle. I asked him to focus on just one person and define a time and place they were together. I continued with the workshop. About half an hour later, I saw a tear in the corner of his eye and a slight smile forming on his lips. He looked at me and said: "Now I remember. Thank you for helping me remember."

Life is never as bleak as many singles lead themselves to believe. Once they define their Inner Circle, they are able to take that first important step toward marriage. Inside there is always a wellspring of wisdom and love waiting to be tapped.

When these memories of personalities brought to life are felt, we begin to touch the side of ourselves which creates the deepest and most precious of all relationships. While the gift may have been initiated from without, it now resides within us. We in turn can give it to others with whom we wish to create a relationship worthy of marriage.

Moving through the seven gates toward marriage requires these feelings and memories that are your inner guide to recognize your *bashert*. This genuine self is deeply and unalterably the true you. I don't mean the professional you, the East Side, West Side, Up Town, Brooklyn, L.A., or even Rechavia you. It's not where you daven, what you wear or what you drive. I am referring to the deepest side of your humanity which can sense and express your most precious feelings. This is what you need to use, skillfully and intelligently, to create a relationship worthy of marriage.

The impact of the Inner Circle can be very striking and immediate. Sholom, a 55 year old single man, had called me to ask for assistance in dating. I first got to know Sholom about 9 months ago when I had given a

VI. Introduction To Your Inner Circle

group for men. I can't tell you what Sholom was like before the group, or how assertive or self confident he felt. He told me he was quite uncomfortable talking to women, both on the phone and certainly on dates. He found the idea of the Inner Circle interesting and began, initially, to use it on phone calls with prospective dates. After a few tries he called me back to report:

"I called this woman for the first time and as usual, I was nervous. I was afraid of being rejected. But I kept on focusing on a feeling from my Inner Circle. It gave me a feeling of confidence. I saw that I could talk to her freely and calmly, not with the insecurity that I've always felt on these phone conversations. Even when I was put on hold for a few minutes, I just felt that it wasn't a personal insult."

For Sholom, this degree of ease was a great personal accomplishment. He was no longer frightened. He loved the new feeling of freedom. He started to feel as if he could now have a chance at developing a relationship. Over the next few months he began to see a woman who had been widowed a few years earlier. Using his Inner Circle to provide him with a core of confidence, he was able to maintain the balance and self confidence he needed to keep the relationship moving forward. Within 3 months, after being alone his entire adult life, he was a *chosson*.

A preliminary phone conversation marks only the very beginning of a relationship. Using your Inner Circle is a process which accompanies you throughout the relationship and beyond, into marriage and family life. It becomes a genuine resource for every meaningful form of personal communication which asks of you to give, be emotionally available, open, reflective and caring. These are the true ingredients to create a bond between two people yearning to become a *Chosson* and *Kallah*.

≡ Discovering The Many Dimensions of Your Inner Circle

Discovering and utilizing your own Inner Circle happens when you focus on specific moments, feelings and memories related to these important people in your life, observing how these memories cavalcade into an ocean of positive associations. Utilizing the Inner Circle in dating is a fascinating experience. You cause a state of inner focus and security in knowing you are cared for and that your life is of value to others. You then use these feelings to value the person you are dating. You once received a gift of inner life, and now you are returning it.

≡ The Inner Focus of Caring

The first element you will discover when you access experiences from your Inner Circle is that these experiences offered you moments that will live inside of you for an eternity. I can remember 27 years ago, going to the Yeshivah to daven and telling the *rosh yeshivah*, Reb Moshe, that my wife just gave birth to our first child, Esti. I had known Reb Moshe just about all my life. He heard the news and his eyes lit up with a warm inner glow that I'll never forget. His *"Mazel Tov"* and *"Brocha"* for all of life's many bounties were delivered with more caring and sincerity that I can ever remember experiencing before. This moment has become a part of my Inner Circle. When I focus on the experience of someone caring about our happiness so genuinely and sincerely, it becomes an inner focus which helps me care for others and judge the sincerity of their caring for me.

❦ *The Focus on "Hakoras Hatov"*

Hakoras hatov is a principle which lies at the heart of Jewish life. It means assuming responsibility for the caring and gifts graciously given by others and returning these gestures in kind when the opportunity arises. This value of *hakoras hatov* was once poignantly demonstrated by a total stranger at a time when I needed it most. I was driving over the George Washington Bridge on Erev Shabbos, headed for the mountains. The hour was quite late. I had been stuck in city traffic and now needed every minute. On the bridge my tire went flat and so did my heart. I couldn't stop to change the tire because there was a patrol car in back of me with a loudspeaker blaring: "Proceed to the end of the bridge! Do not stop on the bridge!" I arrived at the end of the bridge, where the road widened. A car was stopped there, obviously having his own problems. I ran to the trunk and looked for my jack. The driver of the other car came over to me and asked if I needed assistance. He was clearly not Jewish and obviously friendly. I said: "No thanks, it was just a flat." He left and I started to jack up my car. I heard a crack of metal. The jack had broken. Time had run out for me. Suddenly I saw the same man running toward me, smiling and holding a jack. He had been watching me from a distance. He got me jacked up and changed the tire to my car in a flash. Record time. As he was leaving I asked if I could help him. He said he didn't need help. "So why were you stopped there?" I asked. "Oh, I saw you had problems on the bridge and went on ahead to see if I could help."

"Do you always do that?" I asked.

"Oh no," he said. "You see someone did me a great favor the other day and I was just looking for a way to repay it. When I saw you on the bridge in trouble, I figured this was my chance."

Acquiring your inner focus and expressing your *hakoras hatov* create glimpses of the potential of harnessing your Inner Circle. You remember the meaningful deeply personal gifts of others which enabled you to grow and overcome questions, challenges and even crises in your life. You remember the extraordinary moments of closeness and trust these people engendered in you. You also appreciate that their gifts had a *t'nai* — a condition — that someday you will give a similar gift to others. Now, as you date, you can repay these gifts by giving to another person, whether this person is your *bashert* or not. You are creating a relationship by repaying a gift from your past.

This is what Sholom did while waiting so patiently while on hold. He remembered a feeling created by his Inner Circle and it gave him a chance to say to himself: "Sholom, give the woman a chance. Assume that she's really busy with something urgent. Stop taking it so personally." For Sholom, who could never get beyond these feelings, it was a true breakthrough and a revelation. He gave her the benefit of the doubt and this initial call became the basis of a relationship which eventually led to marriage. At every stage of this program. your ability to move forward is based on a deep sense of security within yourself, created by your Inner Circle.

≑ *Visualization to Experience Your Inner Circle*

Feelings associated with your Inner Circle are experienced through an internal focus. It's these feelings which anchor you in the relationship. If you follow these steps many of you will find the right focus and remember that which moved you so deeply at one time in your life.

> 1. *Before you begin, let's get some people together who are a part of your Inner Circle. Try this: Create a list of the people to whom you feel close and with whom you want to share a special moment of your life. Compile a list of the first 5-10 people you would want to give brochos at your wedding, or their counterparts, if they are women. These are people who may have passed on or who are still a part of your life.*
>
> 2. *Select just one person from your list and remember a special moment you shared. (For example, a special moment you remember with a grandparent, parent or teacher with whom you were close.)*

3. Imagine reliving this experience with this person.

4. Remember the place, the face and the feeling within yourself.

5. Hold on to this feeling and try to repeat this exercise when you are alone, when you are davening or saying Tehillim, and start to make this feeling a daily part of your conscious life.
It will become the feeling you will try to recreate as you proceed on to find your bashert even in the middle of Grand Central Station during rush hour.

⚜ *Exercising Your Inner Circle*

If you want to become more comfortable and acquainted with these feelings to incorporate them in your life on a daily basis, then follow these steps.

1. Recreate and re-experience the feelings associated with this member of your Inner Circle.

2. Call a friend to say hello and hold on to the feeling

3. Notice how the content of your communications and even how your voice changes. It becomes softer and more personal. You will also feel more

VI. Introduction To Your Inner Circle

> *understanding, accepting and even reflective.*
>
> *4. Repeat the exercise at work or with family members to whom you want to get closer.*
>
> *5. Remember an experience with your Inner Circle when you take a walk.*
>
> *6. Imagine saying a Brocha or answering Kaddish as if you were reliving this special moment. It adds a very new dimension to inner feelings of Ruchnius and Kavannah.*

These are just a few ways to remember and use the deeper and more delicate side of your emotions, before they were affected by the influences which keep singles apart from their *bashert:* disappointment, the nonsense of Hollywood, professional strivings, family commitments, financial security and all the other forces which contribute to a life of barren loneliness. These special memories are the raw materials of human feelings needed to deeply move you. They are the basis for creating a relationship which leads to love and marriage. With this in place, after you have remembered relived and thought through your Inner Circle, we can now move on to the seven gates leading to marriage.

Only within the power of your Inner Circle can these seven stages be effective in helping you find your life partner. I was called by a young man Kenneth, a successful lawyer. He was dating Susan, a social worker. He desperately wanted to move the relationship forward. He convinced me that he thought she was the one he had been looking for all these years. I helped him get past the first two stages in the program successfully.

Then he called with his own questions. He now had her full interest and caring but he was backing out. He was scared. But, instead of dealing with it, he was pulling the ultimate power play — disappearing. I realized that he was not grounded in real feelings for her. He was playing around, titillating himself and her, until she began to feel something. I had neglected to ground him in the authenticity of his Inner Circle. Because it's only the deeper relationships which once mattered which have the power to take him out of his world of law and acquisitions, competitiveness, victories and defeats, and place him back into a world where people can care for him and he for them. I had neglected to anchor him into the world of whom he is deep inside. Instead he used what I taught him to make her a "conquest." I had given him the ability to "win." The reality was that, in the end, he continued to be a loser and she was treated unfairly.

When you are anchored in your Inner Circle, you leave the world of your emotionally distant self shielded by your profession, status, finances, lifestyle and social airs. The memory of these experiences guarantee that you can not and will not exploit or hurt. On the contrary, you look for avenues to help and give what you have received from others in your life. Dating becomes your George Washington Bridge. You're out to give. And once you're ready to give, you're also ready to learn the seven stages that will bring you *b'ezras Hashem* to marriage.

I met a young man, Paul, who had been the child of an early divorce. After the divorce his mother died. Later in life his sister died. When he married he and his wife constantly fought. They had a child and then divorced. But Paul was strong and determined. He loved his daughter and devoted all his spare time to her upbringing. He couldn't seem to get a relationship going. He was always focused on the superficialities of looks and profession. I realized that he was really saying that loved ones die, so don't love. I anchored him into his Inner Circle. He remembered loving moments with his mother before she died. He started crying. I was relieved because he could access his Inner Circle. Now he could focus on the *pnimius* – the inner side of a person, because he was focused on his own inner dimension.

VII. Seven Gates to the Kingdom of Marriage

☙ The Seven Gates: An Acquisition For A Lifetime

For most singles, years of unsuccessful attempts to find their *bashert* has turned dating into a difficult and disappointing requirement leading nowhere and is best to be avoided. Years go by and mature singles settle deeply into their life styles. A never ending cycle of mixed emotions and confusion reigns as they struggle to fight off that greatest of all fears, that their single lives will not change.

VII. Seven Gates To The Kingdom Of Marriage

This program is determined to create a change in this situation through combining experiences from your Inner Circle while guiding you through seven clearly defined stages toward marriage. Each stage follows the next in deepening the relationship and serves a dual function. First, these stages create appropriate emotional connections between two people which serve as an initial basis for marriage. Second, each stage becomes a testing ground to determine whether the person you are dating has the emotional responsiveness required from a marriage partner. You are essentially determining whether your partner has the "raw material" to be your partner for life. At each stage you create and sustain meaningful emotional bonds between yourselves by casting your precious jewels into the pond of another person's consciousness and then waiting to observe the ripples- those personal responses to your jewels.

Each gate you pass through achieves an emotional depth required for two people to feel that something special and extraordinary is happening. Passing through each gate is a personal acquisition between two people experiencing something special and extraordinary with each other. It's an acquisition because it's a shared achievement, the way you acquire property, knowledge, a law degree, paintings, rare autos, stamps, or anything else in life, both tangible and intangible. But, unlike Kenneth, the lawyer who didn't understand how to acquire levels of commitment, your Inner Circle focuses you on acquiring mutual levels of growth together. With each gate you are acquiring a new meaning of understanding in a relationship of profound emotional meaning.

In this program, the manner in which you acquire is

through giving. What do you give? You give of yourself. Rabbi Eliyahu Dessler זצ״ל understood so well the meaning of acquiring through giving. He provides us with a fascinating analogy. If you would see a man fall off a bridge, but couldn't stop to help him, the next day you might scan the papers to see what ever happened to the poor chap. But, if you saw him hit the water and you jumped in to help him, the next day you would be at his side, nursing him back to life, caring for his needs. When we give to someone, we grow by encompassing the other person. At each stage of this program your orientation is to give in a small, yet highly defined way. After you have given, you wait to observe the response. And in your giving you will have also grown.

You acquire the seven gates by passing through the following steps at each gate:

> *1. Become familiar and comfortable with the memories of your Inner Circle and the many warm and positive feelings they engender in you.*
>
> *2. Carefully understand the concepts and experiences associated with each gate.*
>
> *3. Prepare the necessary jewels in the form of questions and statements before each date.*
>
> *4. Visualize yourself and practice casting jewels, observe the responses.*

5. Actually create an experience with your dating partner.

6. Evaluate the response and move on to the next step.

Following this procedure will bring you closer to marriage.

The First Gate:
The Critical Focus — Hope and Belief

Recently, I had a rude awakening. Channa had been dating Jonathan for a while. With each date Channa reported steady progress and comfort that they were getting closer to making a decision to marry. Jonathan even asked her to call him at work every day and leave friendly voice messages to reassure him that she was thinking of him. They began to see each other daily and discuss issues related to their future lives together as a couple. There was no proposal yet. It was too early for that. But there was a growing security and an understanding that something was happening between them. Channa was waiting for him to be more assertive about marriage. Then Jonathan surprised Channa with an invitation to spend Shabbos together with his Rebbe's family. She felt that this would be the opportunity.

Channa called me with a sense of great excitement. At last she was approaching the chance she'd been waiting for. She planned for this special first Shabbos very carefully. She was determined to make it memorable. On Friday afternoon, as she was planning to join him, she received a phone call from her friend who had made the original introduction. Her friend was conveying a

VII. Seven Gates To The Kingdom Of Marriage

message from Jonathan. "He wants to ease up a bit. It's going too fast." That's all she heard. She went blank. The Shabbos was off, the dream dissolved into a painful reality of searing hurt and disappointment. Once again, she was left out to dry. Of course, there was no longer any contact from Jonathan. For me, witnessing the tragedy was heartbreaking.

Yet, Channa healed and bounced back. Mature singles are resilient that way. They must be stronger than the challenges they continuously face. Within a few weeks she had successfully gone through the gates of a relationship with another young man and felt that a very real opportunity to marry was again approaching. This time, however, she was using herself with greater focus and personal strength. She learned from the pain. We worked together to move through the last stages of the relationship. Each moment was challenging. But she had learned how to balance herself in the wind tunnel of dating. Channa is now a Kallah. Her life will now unfold.

The almost tragic scenario ended in a Simcha. Unfortunately, tragic scenarios like Channa's are neither new or even remarkable. It has become standard fare with mature singles. Just when the relationship appears to have a life of its own, something unexplainable happens and the door is suddenly closed. I was just as baffled as Channa by the phenomenon. The more I analyzed the phenomenon between Channa and Jonathan, as well as other couples, the more I came to understand that at least one member of the couple had to be grounded and locked into in a very powerful inner goal. The Inner Circle is necessary to provide a paradigm of a loving and giving relationship. I later came to understand that this inner goal had to be grounded in internalized images of hope and belief.

What's the difference between hope and belief? Hope is a positive feeling. It's an inner inspiration, a song emerging from deep within us. Hope is a reassuring smile from the heart, a deep breath and certainty that wonderful and precious events will take place in your life.

Belief is a more graphic perception. It's something you actually see and believe in through your mind's eye. It may not be true yet. It's an internal picture based on realities which you believe in and have incorporated through your exposure to other married couples, including your own family. Belief is an image of yourself at your own *chupah*. It's your ability to see yourself in your home with your own family, at a Shabbos table, a birthday party, and anniversary. It's a moment of closeness and love between husband and wife. Hope and belief are the emotional and visual messages with which you reassure yourself that marriage can and will be real, *B'ezras Hashem*.

We have defined hope and belief. Now, what is focus? Focus is a single minded laser sharp perception and determination to hold on to that which is precious in your mind and heart. David Jansen, the gold medal Olympic speed skater revealed that while he was skating around the track he never lost his internal visual focus on the prize. I know stock traders who don't take their eyes off the board the entire day. I know of cardiac surgeons who perform delicate procedures all day long, focused on movements which are as delicate as the stirrings of the very hearts they are healing. I myself have sat and listed to clients in psychotherapy from early

VII. SEVEN GATES TO THE KINGDOM OF MARRIAGE

morning to late at night, focused on every word, gesture and nuance of emotion. All growth and success in life requires focus. Marriage requires this focus.

The mature single has many commitments and points of focus in his or her life. When Channa entered into Jonathan's life he experienced an initial excitement. She loomed large and bright, like the moon at mid-month. She seemed to be the answer he was always looking for. At that moment, there was no doubt. She's the one!

That's why he wanted her to enter his life more fully by calling and dating more frequently. His other commitments fell into the background and she was very prominently on his mind. But, as time passed, the other commitments once again appeared more prominently in his focus and Channa's status as a "full moon" diminished and gave way to other pressing issues. He lost sight of his feelings for her as he began to consider how he would have to rearrange his life. He began to feel overwhelmed and frightened. Perhaps it was the second thoughts that generated fears that "there is someone better." Perhaps it was experiencing a loss of freedom, or even having to share his hard earned assets. Whatever it was, at one moment he was accelerating the pace, the next moment he was applying the brakes. Yes, it's a contradiction. But it's borne out of conflicting allegiances and an inability to maintain a focus on his feelings for Channa and their future.

In the end he pulled the plug in a most inconsiderate and even cruel manner. Certainly, Channa deserved a call, an explanation, an apology. She received none of these. Because for Jonathan, Channa was no longer in focus, no longer a person. She was now a blur, a vague memory, a red flag which told him that if he wanted to protect his precious world, he better run for cover. This is what he did, without any concern for the woman he was considering marrying just a few days before.

For marriage to happen, someone has to hold on securely to the focus, regardless of fears and doubts. Someone in the dating relationship has to be David Jansen, clearly focused on the gold medal, skating against odds and against the agonizing memory that in the competition earlier he had slipped, leaving little hope for the precious gold medal. Now, it was the intensity of his focus which carried him across the finish line to victory. For us, focus on hope and belief that marriage can and will occur is the crucial ingredient. These are our wings to marriage.

Why is hope so important at the beginning of your relationship? Because hope is your response to experiences of hurt and frustration. It heals the wounds of a single still in search of a *bashert*. Hope and belief are important because healthy lives must be fueled and driven by an underlying feeling that we can and will share our lives with another person through love and emotional fulfillment. Hurt and disappointment weaken hope. Without hope, we're lost, like ships without a destination. The saying goes: "Ships without a port are always in a storm." Hope and belief ground us, direct us, strengthen us and give us the port.

In Yiddishkeit we have countless expressions of hope which fill our lives. How many times a day do we say "G-D willing (*Im yertza Hashem*)?" We repeat it day after day throughout our lives. It means that we have the emotional strength to rely on *Hashem* to safely guide us through the storm of life. Unfortunately, this has become an expression frequently devoid of deeper meaning.

Despite the idioms and expressions of hope, mature singles struggle with the challenge to keep hope alive. How well I have come to understand the pain which causes many singles to stop dating or cease to care, because inside they feel a sense of pessimism and disinterest. I recently spoke to a young man, 28, who had been dating for 6 years. He's a respected Ben Torah and has begun to pursue a profession in computer programming. All of a sudden, he's unable to date! It's easier to stay at home, learn and "make better use of his time." To hope is not simply an expression. It wells up from deep within and drives thoughts, feelings and actions. Without it, nothing stirs. With it there is the feeling that life can change.

Pessimism and closing down does not represent a weakness of personality. Rather, it is the accumulation of years of frustration, like water eroding stone. Everyone wears down, even the strongest and most determined. A close friend told me that he never expected to see the pain his twenty three year old daughter was experiencing after going out with more than thirty different young men. I thought to myself: if she was feeling pain, then multiply this number of dates for a mature single who is 30, 35, 40, even 55. As you multiply the number of dates, multiply the pain. The pain and hurt is astronomical. The challenge to continue is staggering. These feelings eventually erode a sense of hope. The personal challenge from fear that life may never be any different, is overwhelming. It is deep and private and no one reveals it very easily.

For marriage to evolve from a new relationship there must be hope. What is hope? It is the promise and belief that life can and will change. Hope is a function of the heart, a state of being, the adrenaline of the soul which moves us forward against the storm.

Rabbi Yechiel Yitzchok Perr שליט״א, Rosh Hayeshivah of Yeshivas Derech Eyson has told the same moving story of hope many times over. He prefers to tell it at the final Seuda for the Yom Tov of Pesach. Chassidim call this the Seuda of Moshiach. Others call it *Neilas HaChag* — the final moments of the Yom Tov. It's when the boys in the Yeshivah gather to celebrate the last meal of the Yom Tov of *geula* — redemption. Pesach is in its waning hours and there is a need for chizuk — emotional strengthening at the thought of leaving Pesach and our shared hope and yearnings for Moshiach and the long awaited redemption of our people.

He tells the story of his *rebbetzin's* late father-in-law, Rabbi Yehuda Leib Nekritz, ז״ל, who had fled the German onslaught from Bialystok and found refuge in Siberia. There he was, stranded, with his family, no means of support, no food and no protection against the brutal winter. It was on a bitter and cold winter morning, at 4:00 AM, that Rabbi Nekritz set out in chest high snow to a neighboring town, hours away. His mission was to stave off starvation by finding a peasant who would be willing to trade his only possession, a precious bar of soap, for a piece of bread. It meant survival.

He left his family in the Siberian night and arrived midday at the town. The entire day he searched in vain for someone willing to make the trade. As the day ended he realized that his mission had failed. He would have to return home without food. Darkness would soon arrive. He made his way, stooped and broken, over the frozen tundra, still holding on to his bar of soap. With no food for his family, his spirit waned, hope was swiftly fading. He knew that when he would arrive home, his children would embrace him out of love and the comforting knowledge that he was safe. But the embrace would also be to see if there was life giving food in his pockets. This was actually told to me by his daughter, *Rebbetzin* Perr, who remembers the poverty and starvation of Siberia vividly.

Making his way over the icy terrain he made out the figure of a peasant. Rabbi Nekritz was alone with no protection. He knew this peasant. He was a gruff and senseless man, even prone to violence. He sensed danger. Who knew what the peasant wanted from him? Still, he had nothing to lose. The goy approached him and screamed out: "Rabbi Nekritz, why are you so broken? Why is your head down? Don't you know that the same G-D who took your people out of Egypt and saved you and your ancestors all these years will save you again?" He never expected to hear these words. He felt a jolt of life and energy surge inside as each word of this peasant as a sign from *Hashem*, entered his being.

He experienced a rekindling of hope and belief, picked up his head, made his way home and survived to bring his family to America. Fifty years later the husband of his daughter speaks of this moment to plant hope in the hearts of yeshivah students bidding farewell to the *Yom Tov* of Pesach. This is hope.

Hope for the mature single is in no way different. It is just as essential to life and the strength to succeed at achieving life's precious goal of love and companionship. Hope and belief ask that you open your mind and heart to the possibility that life can change. As you open up to new dreams, you also open up to new feelings and attitudes toward the way you see and feel about dating and marriage.

Hope creates a vivid, powerful and undeniable certainty in the mind's eye, which becomes the fuel for a new reality in our lives. It changes the way people date. I have a close friend who, tragically, lost his wife after a prolonged illness. After about a year he started going out with a woman who had never been married, but had dated continuously for many years. After 2 months they were engaged. I asked him what enabled him to get married so quickly, especially to a woman who had never succeeded in marrying before. From his answers it was clear that in his mind's eye, there was never any doubt that he would marry. He had been happily married before. He knew it to be a reality and wanted to marry once again. He found the right person, pursued her and finally married her. He was filled with hope and certainty, the rest was having the skills to make marriage a reality.

This feeling of hope and confidence is rarely experienced by mature singles who have never married. I believe there are two essential reasons. The first is that over time, exposure to disappointing relationships erodes hope and belief that anything can ever change. It's a natural consequence. The second reason is that marriage was never a reality for these singles. They have dreams, true. But these dreams are not rooted in life experience and are therefore easy to lose. Marriage is uncertain and untested, unlike the predictability of everyday life as a single, even with all its shortcomings. This weakens hope, because it raises the underlying question of "Is it all worth it?"

Hope is at the heart of all meaningful relationships. It is our emotional lens through which we see the world. With it we are interested in looking into the subtleties of personality character. Hope is our own transmitting tower which creates optimism that life will change, and that our dreams can become a reality.

≣ Locking In Your Focus on Hope and Belief

To date effectively, your first gate is to "lock in" a firm focus on hope and belief. This inner clarity and confidence enables you to continuously assess your partner's maturity and readiness to move forward toward marriage. This focus creates your inner gold standard for what appropriate responses should be. It lets you know rather quickly whether the person you are dating has the same level of drive and interest as you do in marriage.

First Step: Visualizing Hope and Belief

Our first step is to go through a visualization or fantasy of hope and belief. Each of these visualizations will help you access positive internal images and feelings enabling you to clarify your inner focus.

≣ Visualization Of Hope

The visualization of hope centers on a feeling of Bitachon- faith, that *Hashem* has created another person in this world just for you. It's a visualization you can use over and over. Each time you will find it more illuminating and inspiring.

1. Close your eyes.

2. Select someone from your *Inner Circle*

3. Select an experience you have shared together with this person.

4. Focus and hold on to the experience and imagine yourself standing in a dark field at night

5. Look up at a billion stars illuminating the black sky like fine jewels.

6. Feel a closeness to Hashem who has created these stars and given each its own name.

7. Look closely among the stars until you can see one star shining brighter than the rest. Realize this is your star. It is peering down at you, shining for you, caring for you. It represents your specialness and uniqueness in all the world.

8. As you look even closer at the billion stars in the heavens, you can see another star shining with equal intensity. Two stars shining above a billion

9. Realize that this illuminated star represents your *bashert*. It is a message from Hashem that there is indeed another soul

created and so uniquely suited for you. And you for him or her.

10. *Feel a sense of hope slowly grow inside of you. You may sense it through a gentle tear or as you take a deep breath. These are signs of your sense of hope reawakening in you.*

11. *Say: "Thank You Hashem for placing another person in the world who is my bashert. I believe I will find this person and together we will share our lives.*

≑ *Visualization: Belief – The Chupah*

The second visualization is belief - your ability to believe that one day you will be standing next to your *bashert* at your chupah.

1. *Close your eyes*

2. *Select a person from your Inner Circle*

3. *Select an experience you have shared together with this person and focus on to the feelings associated with this experience.*

4. *While holding on to the experience, imagine you can see a bride and groom walking toward you. They radiate love and*

joy at the knowledge that their lives will be spent together.

5. As they approach, you realize that it is yourself whom you see. Alongside is your *bashert*.

6. There are many people who have gathered around both of you. Each wishes you a Mazel Tov from their hearts and shares true joy in your Simcha.

7. You can make out faces of people past and present, hugging you and expressing their joy.

8. You are under the *chupah*. Your eyes are filled with the whiteness of flowers and purity.

With this vision you can feel the resurgence of belief that this will one day be your true *chupah*.

≑ *Integration —* *Getting Focus Into Your Life*

Now that you have visualized hope and belief, the next step is to learn how to integrate focus into your life on a daily basis.

You integrate focus by gradually learning to productively use time designated for both serious reflection and even relaxation and leisure to deepen your internalization and understanding of the feelings related to hope and belief. When you use these moments to your advantage, you will find a gradual integration and comfort with this focus — as if it were second nature. You will be able to remember its importance and you'll be able to hold on to important ideas, images and feelings, so very much needed as you proceed toward marriage.

Here are some of the moments of intense concentration and leisure you will learn to use toward the integration of your focus:

1. Davening

Because we strive for concentration and reflection during Davening, it's a perfect time to focus on these feelings. While Davening, try to imagine yourself at your own *chupah*, particularly while you are answering to Kaddish, Kedusha and other Tefillos which evoke emotions. You will find that two effects are immediately recognizable. First, you will experience your Davening as more intense and clear and your *Kavannah* will increase. Second, through your focus while Davening you will feel a deepening of your focus in your hope and belief in marriage.

2. While Saying Brochos

Use *Brochos* as a means to strengthen your hope and belief that *Hashem* will fulfill your desire, which is also *Hashem's* desire, as well.

3. While walking or jogging,

Use this leisure time to concentrate on feelings and images. Try this method. Pick a spot in the distance on which to focus. It can be a tree, a pole, a cloud. Walk ahead while using this point of visual contact to focus on hope and belief. You will find that as you hold the visual contact you will also hold on to the internal focus, as well.

There are many such opportunities which permit you to integrate these feelings. Your ability to succeed in this program is dependent on holding on to your own personal life focus of what your dating and communications are all about. Without the focus you will consistently slip back into unclarity and helplessness, all disguised in many forms. The next six levels are actually all secondary to this first and primary level. Be careful to remember that at each level your success depends on holding on to this focus.

II. The Gate of Affirmation

The gate which actually begins the creating of a relationship is affirmations. Affirmations are the primordial bud, the first blossom, the kernel of all growth. Let's understand how we grow in life. What we are and know on a deeply personal level comes from gifts of caring and *chesed* we have received from those who have loved and thought about our needs over the years, both emotional and physical. From the moment we opened our eyes to the world, learning to speak, walk, even think, all human consciousness is the result of caring. It starts with the gentle and life giving interactions between mother and child during life's earlier years. And it extends on to the complexities of mature love and mutual responsibility for each other's lives and the lives of our children. We learn every one of these skills because we were loved and cared for.

This second gate is the foundation of personal giving. It's the ability to present a gift by symbolically saying to someone: "You are a valued and esteemed person in my eyes." These are affirmations we give to another person. Of course you are not going to say this directly, at least not at the beginning of a relationship. Your focus will be directed on their strengths, values, Midos (personal traits) and other reasons which affirm their life style, values and personality.

Affirmations reinforce our feeling of wholeness and self esteem. They enable us to be and feel the best of who we are. Through them we come to understand that there is "someone who has the ability to recognize and thereby communicate with these positive feelings within me." This creates a special bond between yourself and the individual who affirmed you as a person. The results are undeniably apparent. If you give it some thought you will see that you still harbor warm and fond memories for just about every person who has ever affirmed something about you. It could be a parent, teacher, colleague, employer, rabbi- anyone and everyone.

It can even be small and insignificant things. I remember, during my childhood illness, which I mentioned before, I was kept away from family and friends for long periods. It frequently left me feeling isolated, forgotten and deprived. The end result was a sense of depression and low self esteem. Any gesture toward me which countered this perception was deeply appreciated and remembered until this very day over 40 years later. For this reason I still remember a small gift I received from an aunt, while I was in the hospital. It was a shirt. A short sleeve white shirt with green stripes. I remember unwrapping it. The feel of the tissue paper and the pins which I took out carefully, one by one. I put that shirt on with more pride than I would feel today stepping into a luxury car or a new home. Someone remembered me and made me feel whole. Whenever I wore that shirt I felt it saying: "You really are someone who is worthy of this gift." The shirt affirmed something about me and the memory lingers 43 years later. Affirmations therefore are, in fact, gifts that others have given to us and which we then give to others.

Words are even more important as gifts. They are the first crucial interactive gate because they are expressed as a verbal message directed at affirming a person's dedication in life.

VII. Seven Gates To The Kingdom Of Marriage

Affirmations are a way of saying: "I am interested in seriously exploring a relationship with you and I am ready to start at this moment." Through your message you have set the tone and focus of your relationship. Therefore, at the beginning of the relationship you are in effect saying: "We don't know each other yet. But, I am aware of a principle which guides all relationships, both yours and mine. I affirm in you that which is the center and core of your life's ambitions and values, and I have set a relationship between us into motion."

You are not saying I'll compliment you and you will compliment me. This is empty flattery which is okay for an insincere filler. Affirmations communicate with the deepest and most precious strivings of a person and you express your sincere esteem for these strivings.

I once had the good fortune of having a Chavrusa (study partner) with Rabbi Yisroel Heiman זצ"ל — a Tzaddik and true Talmud Chochom. Reb Yisroel taught second grade girls for more than twenty years and he devoted his life to preparing these young children to become Bnos Yisroel. He could have taught in any yeshivah in the country, at any level. But this is what he devoted himself to. I remember that he had a closet in his house that his own children always treated with awe and respect and would never approach. It was in this closet that Reb Yisroel kept the candies and toys that he gave out as prizes to his 2nd grade girls. These were the rewards used to help them feel good and positive about themselves. He would always say that if he could make the correct impact at this stage in their lives, then it would last a lifetime as they grown into B'nos Yisroel able to share their lives with their own husbands and children. Despite the many offers from Yeshivas throughout the country and the promise of being revered, even possibly as a *rosh yeshivah*, Reb Yisroel stayed on year after year dedicated to creating an impact on 2nd grade girls. For many, his influence would be remembered throughout their student years and even on to building their own families. It was just as he had wanted.

To Reb Yisroel, an affirmation would be: "You have made an impact on the lives of countless B'nos Yisroel because of your dedication to being their 2nd grade teacher." Once this was said you had a friend for life. Because it spoke to the heart of what was so dear and important to him. Anything else skirted the true issue of who this person was and what he wanted to be recognized for.

I am always asked at workshops what an affirmation is. It could be that your are a great athlete, skier, accountant, or Baal *chesed*. My answer has always been: "If you can write it on a person's tombstone, it's an affirmation." It's only those strivings that are inherently related to the everlasting work of Hashem. This is what creates a relationship through affirmation.

Understand clearly that it's no different when you want to tell a dating partner that you are ready to seriously explore the possibility of a relationship which could lead to marriage. It's not a commitment to marry. It is a commitment to take a relationship seriously by taking what a person has done with their life seriously.

Maybe your dating partner teaches 2nd graders; is a social worker for the elderly; or even cares enough about aging parents to call them every day. All these are the basis and a reason for an affirmation. And every affirmation of this type creates an impact, deep within and becomes the foundation of a true relationship. This affirmation which communicates so deeply is the very first jewel you cast into the pond. And this jewel creates a ripple on the surface of the waters. The ripples for Reb Yisroel would be a warm smile of appreciation that someone understood and valued why he had devoted his life to these young girls.

What are the ripples you see in your dating partner when you affirm something of value in their lives? It may be a smile, a softening of the tone, a returned affirmation, or some other positive gesture which says: "Thank you for appreciating me." You may also want to ask yourself: "How did I feel about giving you the affirmation? And if you acknowledged it, how did this effect me? In short what were the ripples created in you and in myself?"

Through affirmations you achieve two important milestones right at the beginning of a relationship. First, you are creating a connection through your gift of affirmations. On dates, very few meaningful gifts are exchanged. Second, by providing your gift and observing the ripples, you are determining whether your partner understands the meaning of receiving and accepting affirmations. It tests your partner's ability to accept and acknowledge that someone appreciates and values important areas in their life and lifestyle. You are actually saying in an indirect way: "I feel that you make right choices in your life, therefore I respect and value you as a person."

Choosing specific areas to affirm before a date or

phone call enables you to cast your jewels and observe the response. The results are always surprising. Because affirmations bypass the guards people put up to protect themselves against exposure and vulnerability. The correctly worded affirmation causes synapses to jump and at times, sparks to fly. And it doesn't require a poetic or dramatic affirmation, nor a dynamic personality. The dynamism is contained in the lifetime of inner hopes and dreams that each person carries into the date- the dream to be emotionally moved when they are recognized as a genuine and truthful person, by another genuine and truthful person.

❦ *The Surprise of Fascination*

Affirmations provide dates with their inherent power. Their power is tapped by your readiness and ability to nurture, appropriately and at the right time. When they register, the effect can be fascinating, even for those we may see as uncomplex and "simple."

Moshe had attended a seminar I had given. About a month after the seminar he called for advice regarding a date. Moshe always felt uncomfortable on dates. He was about to date a woman for the second time, which for him was a rarity. He rarely got to a second chance. She seemed to be different than the other women he had dated. She was a special education teacher, who had devoted her professional career to helping children with learning disabilities. He very much wanted to proceed, but experience taught him that whatever he would say would somehow backfire. Much like my batting career

VII. SEVEN GATES TO THE KINGDOM OF MARRIAGE

as a youngster, for Moshe, dates contained the promise of only failure.

It was clear that his date was a woman who had dedicated much of her life to her special learning needs students. It was important for Moshe to understand that when a person dedicates so much of her life to helping handicapped children, she values being appreciated for this dedication. This was the most effective way of demonstrating his serious intention to get to know her. I said: "Listen, Moshe. Forget for a moment that you are looking to marry. This woman has devoted her life to these kids. If you were her, wouldn't it be great if someone came along and affirmed this devotion and commitment and really meant it?" Moshe was surprised and even put off: "You want me to tell her that before I even know her?"

"Moshe," I said, "if you don't start now you'll never know her and she'll be just another woman who slipped away."

Moshe was amazed at the boldness of the move I was asking him to make. Faced with certain failure, he agreed. Together, we fashioned a script, of sorts, which enabled him to express both admiration for her dedication and questions related to her students. While we worked out the wording, the sentiments were genuinely his.

He went on his date and got back to me a day later. He couldn't suppress his excitement. Something wonderful and totally unexpected had happened. He wasn't prepared for such expressiveness and enthusiasm. He was well into his 50s and never had a date express herself so openly and spontaneously to him before. All he did was express his affirmation about how impressed he was at the level of dedication she demonstrated to her students and she started sharing the most important aspect of her life. He was enthralled and listened intently. He wasn't putting on the interest. He really was fascinated. In all the years of his dating he never experienced fascination.

It reminded me of a bag of candy we had brought to a Yeshivah family living in extremely modest physical conditions in Yerushalyim. Every penny was accounted for in making ends meet. The mother, an old friend of ours, carefully took out a red lollipop from the bag and gave it to her 4 year old son. He looked at it almost oddly, slowly took off the wrapper and placed it on his tongue. Suddenly, his eyes lit up, like the jackpot on a slot machine and a huge smile broke on his face. He was literally aglow. "He never had candy before," his mother said. That explained everything.

Moshe had never tasted fascination before. All the while he kept on asking himself: "Did I really get this started?" Not only was he interested, he was deeply moved by her dedication and sincerity. Suddenly his string of failures was not his focus. There was an interesting and very vital human being who was expressing herself to him and he was truly and sincerely enraptured by what she was saying and how she was saying it. He didn't yet realize that he was just scratching the surface. This was only the beginning. What Moshe learned was that he could cast a jewel into the pond and be fascinated by the ripples that he alone created. It was an exhilarating experience.

Moshe could have gone out with this woman many times, worn the same clothing, gone to the same places, ordered the same meal, but nothing would have clicked.

VII. SEVEN GATES TO THE KINGDOM OF MARRIAGE

He would be rejected and wait patiently until the next date and the next rejection. One slight modification and it all changed. What is clear is that Moshe communicated deeply with this woman. It was an issue around which she has dedicated her life. Had it not been touched upon, there would never have been any basis for their communication.

Sometimes we deal with people who are more complex and reflective. It takes them a while to process what happens on a date, especially after they share their gifts with someone. Consider what happened to Mark and his about-face:

Meir had his first date with Devorah. He was a brilliant Maggid Shiur in a Mesivtha. Devorah was a receptionist from a well known family with an excellent educational background. Both were in their mid 30s. He had attended one of my workshops and took my advice about affirmations rather seriously. Before the date he did his homework, got the information and prepared the affirmations. He had learned that she was active in many community *chesed* organizations and used whatever he learned to transmit his impression that she was a thoughtful and giving person. Then a strange thing happened. She was overwhelmed by his verbal gifts. It was the first time in her life anyone had ever treated her this way.

He, on the other hand got scared. He had spilled out too much and too many exchanges had transpired between them. He was frightened that he had over-committed himself too early before he knew her well enough. She called the Shadchon and said: "He's a wonderful person, unlike any one I have ever met." He called the same shadchon and said: "She's a very nice girl, but I'm not really sure." The Shadchon was upset and called me. I told her to relax and give it a couple of days. Meir went to sleep and had a chance to think through the date. He woke up in the morning excited. He began to understand that she heard and understood everything he said. He started to reconstruct her responses and gestures and realized he had never gone out with such a deep and special girl. He then realized that he may have made a mistake and led the Shadchon to believe that he wasn't interested. Perhaps this was shared with Devorah. He immediately called and said: "I hope you didn't say anything to her. I had a chance to think it over. I must admit she really is a special person."

These affirmations occurred relatively early in a relationship. When they occur later in a relationship, their impact can be almost cataclysmic. Consider the following events which took place between Lillian and Barry.

The couple had been dating on and off for a few months. They moved through gates and their relationship was deepening and becoming more focused and solidified. However, Lillian had been asking Barry for one very important level of commitment. He had been earning a relatively low salary as a bookkeeper. But he loved the company, the people and the routine of his employment. The problem was that it was a dead end company and a dead end job. He had shown promise with computer skills, but never acted on them. Lillian encouraged him to enroll in an advanced computer course which would enable him to provide an adequate income. Until now he had been reticent. One day he announced that he enrolled in the program. She was elated.

I suggested that Lillian affirm Barry's demonstration

of commitment through a card and a small gift, perhaps a piece of candy. This was her way of affirming and showing her appreciation, without going overboard and frightening him.

She sent him a card and a small candy gift as a token of affirmation. He responded the next day by saying he wanted to thank her for her thoughtfulness. It meant a lot to him. He suggested that they have dinner together. As they dined he said that he had a card for her, as well. He took out a card with a beautiful expression of his own appreciation. She read it and was deeply moved. Then he took out a bracelet and asked her to be his wife. She cried and accepted his wonderful offer.

Perhaps his proposal would have come at this time and place. Yet, consider the affirmation which says: "I appreciate you and what you are." Consider how a blossoming of relationships becomes so much easier and more natural.

✠ *Levels Of Affirmation*

Affirmations mean that you verbally express your esteem and value of someone, either directly or indirectly. To make this statement means stepping out on a limb. The degree to which you step out on a limb depends on how direct and personal the affirmation is. Basic affirmations are those which value some general aspect of the person's life style. For example: "I'm really impressed that you spend so much time preparing for your class." It is easier for the recipient to accept this general affirmation without feeling that they are making a premature commitment to the relationship.

More personal affirmations used later in a relationship require greater risk and commitment. They may contain an element of time, such as : "I have always looked for a person with the kind of personal integrity you possess." Therefore, depending on which stage you are in a relationship, affirmations can be expressed on numerous levels. Each should be used at their appropriate times.

I have defined 4 levels of affirmations.

Level 1. Affirming the Lifestyle

This is the safest level because it does not relate to either party directly and will not lead to any embarrassment or feelings of being prematurely direct. These are excellent for first dates. Essentially they let your date know that you have thought about them and you value what they have done with their lives:

- *I am fascinated with your dedication as a teacher*
- *I have a great deal of respect for your decision to befriend someone who desperately needs your friendship.*
- *I know and have high regard for so many people whom you choose to Daven with, and particularly the Rov.*
- *I feel your school is making a great contribution to Torah in America.*
- *It's very commendable that you take time off from work to learn*

Level 2. Affirming the Person

This is a more direct level and touches on the person him/herself. It should be used at a more advanced stage of the relationship and runs the risk of causing embarrassment if used too prematurely. Essentially, it sends the message to your date that you admire the qualities of their personality:

- *I admire the fact that you have cultivated a very special way of expressing yourself.*
- *I admire your commitment to chesed.*
- *You appear to be a very dedicated teacher.*
- *I am impressed by your sincere and serious way of expressing yourself.*

Level 3. Expressing the Personal Impact on Yourself

The most impactful level of affirmation includes yourself in the compliment. It not only makes a statement about the person, but also tells this person what their qualities mean to you. This level means greater certainty on your part that the relationship is serious and greater security that the recipient is ready to hear and feel the mutual impact of the affirmation.

Here are some even more advanced affirmations:
- *Thinking of you reminds me of what it's like to be a caring person*
- *I must say that you bring out a feeling of security in me.*

- *Your optimism brings out my best qualities.*
- *I feel a greater sense of joy and hope when I think of you.*
- *I am inspired by your sense of commitment.*

Level 4. Affirmations Which Imply Commitment

The final level of affirmation tells this person that based on this impact you are ready to commit yourself. It differs from the previous level in that it contains the element of time.

- *I have always looked for a person with your sense of optimism.*
- *Ever since I have begun dating, I have looked for someone with your personal commitment to Yiddishkeit.*

≑ *Preparing Your Affirmations*

Preparing your affirmations requires that you do some initial homework. Find out all you can about your date's life style, including:

- *Approximate age*
- *Education*
- *Income source*
- *Family background*
- *Social and religious relationships*

VII. Seven Gates To The Kingdom Of Marriage

Proceed onto the important issues which will help you prepare affirmations including:

- *What are the major chesed activities of this person?*
- *What are their abiding social and community interests?*
- *Who are the families, community leaders, Rabbonim and rebbetzins to whom this person is closest?*

You will build your affirmations based on those issues which relate to the deeper side of your dating partner's life.

Once you have used affirmations on a date, it's time to observe the "ripples" as verbal and physical gestures of acknowledgment, as well as how it feels for you to share the affirmations. These ripples will help you determine whether this person is capable of being a warm and giving person, something you should know at this early stage of dating.

≉ *Affirmations — In Conclusion*

Through affirming, you have set the very first foundation of a relationship in place which can lead to marriage. Through your statement you have said: "I don't know you very well. Neither do you know me. I do know, however, that in order for both of us to attempt to deepen our relationship, we must treat that which is most important in our respective lives with utmost respect and dignity. Therefore I am offering you a gift through admiring that which is most important to you in your life." You offer this gift and observe the ripples you have created through your affirmation. These ripples, as expressed by a smile, a note of gratitude, tell you that you have been heard, that your gift has been received and appreciated. Therefore you want to proceed on to the next gate of your relationship.

III. The Gate of Inner History

You have offered your affirmations and you have a positive feeling about the relationship. You are ready to proceed. Your next gate is to open up the inner history.

What's an inner history? It's asking a question that gives you a chance to know a person from the inside and in a way that you are ready to listen with a serious focus. Because it tells you something about the life of the other person and yourself.

Earlier in this book I wrote how my fist attempt to listen with this inner ear occurred when I was in my early 20s and realized that I had so many questions to ask my grandfather, Reb Dovid Sohn, who lived in Boston. I had to know what was it like coming from Europe to Boston, bringing up a Frum family in a Catholic city, surviving a car accident which killed his wife and left him a widower to raise his family alone. There were endless questions that I had to ask. I was so gripped by the fear that I would lose the opportunity forever. So I traveled to Boston the next day and spent the next few days close to him. These days will remain with me for the rest of my life. I began to hear his inner history, and gain a glimpse of how he found the strength to rebuild life over and over. These are the moments which bring people together.

Questions about inner history don't necessarily have to be so profound. They can yield interesting tales. For instance, I can say that I was trained as a social worker or family therapist. You would say: "Okay, he's a social worker." But if you asked me how I became a social worker, I would tell you an interesting story. In 1968 I was attending an evening graduate program in biology, while supporting my family by working for the Department of Social Services. I was approached by a supervisor and asked to take on a caseload of drug addicts in the Bedford Stuyvesant section of Brooklyn. Hardly a place for a young Frum student of biology. I could have objected, but I went along.

After a couple a months of learning how to survive on the job, I was noticed by an off-beat and scruffy looking senior supervisor, Miss Dolgren (then there was no Ms. and I can't remember her first name). Miss Dolgren, who looked and acted like a lumberjack, began to show keen interest in my work with the addicts, of whom she was particularly protective. Miss Dolgren came from Maine and acted as if she drove in from the back woods every morning. She wore big boots, a plaid lumber jacket, close cropped hair, and no makeup. Her appearance seemed to be an emphatic statement of her identification with life in the back woods of Maine. Her non-conformist ways clearly contributed to her determination to give addicts the quality of treatment which would help them recover. While I didn't take my work with the addicts seriously, Dolgren did. To her I was the most skilled caseworker with addicts she had ever seen. She was determined to make sure that I was recognized and rewarded.

At that time the New York City Department of Social Services had a small number of scholarships to social work graduate schools, offering free tuition and full salary. It was a dream deal and was limited to a blessed few.

VII. SEVEN GATES TO THE KINGDOM OF MARRIAGE

Dolgren moved mountains to get me that scholarship. It was unsolicited, unexpected and changed the direction of my life. This is a small piece of my inner history. You would only find out about it if you asked me: "Shaya, how did you become a social worker?"

Learning about someone's inner history is the foundation of getting to know who they are. Many singles never really get to know the people they are dating, because after years of dating there is a tendency to say: "By now, I know exactly what I want. I can make up my mind based on data and a minimum of information." The end result is that the data and information are substituted for the person. They never get to know the inner history.

Every person has a deep and fascinating inner history. Developing a relationship is getting to know this deeper side. Imagine that you knew Michael, a nondescript, lethargic and generally poorly coordinated kid, from your high school days. He was the kind of classmate who was always the outcast, left behind, continuously failing at all the important things in life. Let's say his family's finances were meager. Imagine that you befriended Michael and attempted to help him, but rarely succeeded. Over the years you lost contact with him and once in a while asked yourself how Michael could have survived in such a competitive world. When thinking of him you always imagined the worst.

Twenty years later your paths cross and you meet. You are overwhelmed and amazed to see that he is now a well groomed, quick witted, highly charged financially and socially successful individual. If you had never known him, you would assume that he had it in his blood. You would assume that he was brought up with all the advantages of a successful family and natural talents which lead to success. But you know the real past and that he had none of these working for him. You would certainly be surprised, even amazed to see the final product. You would want to ask : "Michael, what happened to you. What turned your life around? I never expected to see you like this." You would want to hear the story of his transformation. And as he shared his success story with you, you would hang on to every detail. You would want to know his inner history.

I was once driving through the *Shtachim* — the territories, *Yehuda* and *Shomron* in Israel, when I saw a soldier hitchhiking. He was *Dati* and wore a large knitted *Yarmulke.* He had long *Payos* and appeared as if he had been learning in Yeshivas all his life. He told me that he had 10 children and as was living in a caravan in one of the settlements. Then he told me that he had a attended a secular high school. It seemed utterly incongruous. I asked him, "Who influenced you to become Frum?" He told me, Hashem. How? He entered the army after high school. He was assigned to guard duty in the desert. Neither he nor his parents were Dati. He was assigned to guard duty at night in a desert army camp. At first he detested it. Then, when he got used to the darkness and the long lonely nights he began to watch the stars. One night he was transfixed by the stars and asked himself: "Who created all this?" Night after night, he returned to his stars and his questions about life and the universe. He started to ask people he knew about his questions until he came across a rabbi from one of the local yeshivas who gave him some Seforim to read. Within 6 months he

VII. SEVEN GATES TO THE KINGDOM OF MARRIAGE

was *Frum, Davening,* studying Torah and starting life over again as a *Frum* Jew. This is a piece of inner history.

Chaya is a 33 year old single woman. She was about to date a man who friends had told her "is not her type." She decided to proceed anyway. A phone conversation with him "reconfirmed" what her friends had already warned her. But at this late stage she couldn't pull out without hurting his feelings. So she arranged the "throw away" date and wanted to get over with it as painlessly as possible.

She called me on another matter and happened to discuss the upcoming "disaster." I suggested to her that since she was dating anyway, why not make it an enjoyable date. I suggested a method of taking an inner history, without letting on that I had my own agenda for the suggestion. I was interested, of course, in seeing whether it was possible to turn things around, or at least move Chaya away from her determined sense of gloom about the date.

She told me that her date was a musician. I suggested that she play along with a fantasy. The fantasy is that she had known him in high school and remembered distinctly that he was flat out tone deaf, couldn't hold a note for anything. The kind of guy, who if he sang along with everyone, then everyone just had to stop singing. With this in mind, she has many questions to ask him about what created the turnaround. And the questions would have to be asked with great surprise and interest: "You! You're a musician? How in the world did you do it? What was your secret? Who were your teachers? Don't I recall that you had a hard time holding a note?"

Obviously these weren't the questions. But this was

the tone I suggested in a determined effort to understand how this young man became a musician. She called me after the first date. It's true that there were many differences between them, but she would certainly go out with him again. And they did!

What a wonderful and unexpected surprise when a date works out to be so much better than you thought it would. It doesn't even matter whether this person is destined to be your bashert. What matters is that life can still be a surprise that makes you say: "I'm glad I got to know this person." By telling her to go to the deeper inside story, the deeper dimension of the person, I knew the stereotypes would dissolve and be forgotten. They gave way to a sense of the real and true person, talking to the true you. It's an encounter between two honestly searching people who are both ready to hear and accept the internal signals that they may just be meeting the right person for the first time.

When someone calls to see if you are interested in dating, what are some of the questions you ask to determine whether a date has potential? Of course you will ask about personality, age, height, weight, and other personal and physical features, such as:

- *Where does he (she) work?*
- *Where does he daven?*
- *Where does she live?*
- *What school did he go to?*
- *Does she have a TV?*
- *What about movies, Daf Yomi, etc.*

All these and similar questions are essential in

determining whether a prospective date falls within your guidelines. Knowing a profession, address, affiliations, or interests merely gives you symbols, not the true measure of a person. What is truly important is to understand how a person evolved in life, who and what guided them and directed them to become who they are. Because relationships require a deeper understanding of what drives, motivates and inspires someone.

The inner history achieves two essential goals which form the foundation of any relationship. First it encourages a person to open up, reveal the secret journey that was taken, who and what guided the journey and discloses that beneath the trappings there is a living breathing heart and soul. It reveals that life's decisions are made with great care, thought and feeling. Mostly, it can show you that your dating partner is a reflective person. Why reflective? Because it's this reflective side of a person which enables your partner to experience caring and even love at some time in the future. You very much want to see, hear and feel that reflective side in the ripples you create by your questions.

Second it creates an atmosphere of fascination and education. You as the listener will either be fascinated, educated, or both. If you succeed in touching the inner history, your perception of this person and your relationship will have reached a new level of understanding and insight. It will never be the same. You now have an understanding of just how reflective, thoughtful and focused this person is. If an inner history shows a thoughtful appreciation for life's direction and meaning, then this is a clear indication that this person will be a serious partner for your future family.

Looking at the deeper history can also lead to a surprise. Boruch had been dating Malka, who had a degree in accounting and worked for an accounting firm. He liked many things about her, but he stereotyped her as being too stiff, especially as a wife. The thought of marrying a CPA left him cold. I encouraged him to understand why and how Malka decided to become an accountant. He finally approached her with the question of what and who motivated her to go for a CPA. She told him that the field was the furthest thing from her mind. In fact, she had started as a teacher in a seminary, which she loved doing. However, she wanted to marry someone who would spend time in learning and wanted to find employment which gave her a chance to make more money, greater flexibility and the chance to work at home. She had a friend who was able to maintain a family and practice accounting out of her home. She thought that it could work for her once she was married and had a family. Once he heard the inner history, his perception of Malka was immediately transformed. This is the goal of the inner history.

☙ Preparing Your Inner History Questions

The inner history is an exploration to find common threads that fascinate and bind two people together in the sharing of their lives. It's a search for inspiring moments and people who guide life's decisions. It tells you about a person's deeper values, memorable personalities, forks in the road and how they were taken. Asking about this history is not a commitment to a relationship, but, rather a commitment to enable a relationship to open up and unfold based on whom a person is deep inside. You are saying: "I have asked because I am ready to listen and be moved, enchanted, enthralled and interested in your life and the journey you have taken." For your dating partner, it's a chance to express and share what few people have ever asked. It's an opportunity to share those missions for which they are *"Moser Nefesh"* (deeply committed). These are those special commitments which give their lives meaning and a deeper dimension. It's the chance to talk about great personalities, memorable moments and their crowning achievements in life. These are not expressed out of vanity, but, as a result of responses to your honest and sincere interest.

To prepare your "inner history" questions, develop questions which deal with the personal side of life issues. You can ask such questions as:

1. *Do you remember your favorite teacher?*

2. *What do you enjoy most about Rabbi Gross's shiur?*

3. *Do you remember the first family you ever spent Shabbos with?*

4. *What was it like on your first day of medical school?*

5. *What is it like being the only Shomer Shabbos person in your unit?*

6. Who inspired you to become a psychologist?

7. Do you remember your grandparents?

All these questions and countless others like them open up the door for sharing the inner history.

Your jewels will be questions which encourage your date to open up and reveal a deeper side. I have found that the questions which present the greatest opportunity are those which relate to relationships which have influenced life decisions.

✢ *Inner History — In Conclusion*

Remember that your image of whom your bashert is exists only in your mind and has absolutely no bearing at all to reality. Reality is listening with fascination and deep interest as you hear an inner history which tells you this person is reflective, sincere, sensitive and thoughtful. When you are ready to ask the questions which give that deeper sense and insight, then you are ready to proceed in your relationship onto the next gate of Human Vulnerability.

The Gate of Human Vulnerabilities

Your Inner Circle has guided you through Hope, enabled you to Affirm another person and has directed you to ask the kinds of questions that lead to an opening up of an Inner History. By now you have experienced significant moments of emotional connection toward developing a relationship solid enough to lead to marriage. This next gate is perhaps the most challenging of all the gates. It requires a core of inner strength and trust in yourself and your dating partner.

These initial stages have been devoted to strengthening yourself and determining the emotional strengths of caring and openness in your dating partner. This next gate is devoted to understanding what happens when you show moments of weakness and vulnerability. What will your partner do or say to either assuage your vulnerability or intensify it, even to the point of exploitation. This is a crucial question to ask at this stage because your success in marriage depends greatly on mutual respect for each other's vulnerabilities.

After many years as a marital therapist and even more years as a husband, I have come to understand that sensitivity to vulnerability is the true cement in marriage. When you have shown this vulnerability, you are essentially exposed. You can now ask:

"How will my weakness be heard?"

"What will be the response?"

"How will it effect our relationship?"

"Will they view it as an opportunity to attack me or to respect and value my courage and openness?"

Perhaps this is why *Chazal* — Sages, place the *Mezuzah* on a slant. It is a compromise between two conflicting Halachic opinions as to whether the *Mezuzah* is placed horizontally or diagonally. The result is that it must reflect both angles. The same with marriage. Both partners have to bend to each other for a house to become a home. That's why your vulnerability is such an important element in the relationship. It gives your dating partner a chance to yield and you a chance to experience the yielding of another person just because you are deserving of the consideration.

We are bred in a different world where weakness is deadly. The world of human interaction has to be contrasted with the sharks of business. On a business level, I remember once opening up my financial and emotional vulnerability to a business partner after a very difficult period in my life. His response was to devour me. In our personal life we couldn't survive if this were the response of our friends and relatives. Yet, we must contrast this vulnerability in a highly competitive world to exposing our vulnerabilities in those special relationships between ourselves and others with whom we want to be closer. There can never be closeness without some exposure of vulnerability, because we can never know what the response would be to our expressed weakness.

Probably the most important and historically important incident of human vulnerability related by the Torah happens when Tamar tells Yehudah that he, in fact, has fathered the fetus inside her. She tells him in private. He can admit it to be his and spare her life. Or he can shield himself by publicly insisting that she has illegitimately had relations with another man, and end her life. She has exposed herself and is very vulnerable. His response is to admit his role, spare her life and set the stage, some 400 years later, for the birth of *Dovid Hamelech*. Her vulnerability gave rise to the monarchy which would distinguish our people from among all the nations throughout civilization, through *Dovid Hamelech*, *Tehillim*, the *Bais Hamikdosh*, *Shlomo Hamelech*, *Shir Hashirim* and eventually, *Moshiach*.

It's never easy to expose our vulnerability. It can be a frightening challenge. I vividly remember the vulnerable role I once put myself into for an acquaintance. It was *Erev Yom Kippur* when was I preparing my *Tshuvah* for the next day. My mind focused on an incident I saw a few months earlier. I was in Shul, attending a *Shiur*. Following the *Shiur*, I overheard a heated discussion between two of the Shul's members. One was an investment banker and the other a successful, yet somewhat simple businessman. The banker had a reputation for being a serious Jew. He Davened with intense *Kavanah*, studied Torah regularly and was a generous *Baal Tzedakah*. He was one of the more important and powerful members of the *Kehilla*, with a reputation for brilliant business sense and a violent temper to match. The discussion between the two started to heat up and develop into an argument. It was a mismatch. The banker tore the other member to shreds with sharp, cutting and piercing invectives. The other man walked off in absolute defeat and humiliation.

For some reason I couldn't get this scene out of my mind on *Erev Yom Kippur*. Then I realized what I was saying to myself: "It's *Yom Kippur* tomorrow. I was a witness to this terrible event. I saw it happen. The banker is going into *Yom Kippur*, ready to fast and ask *Hashem* for *tshuvah*. But I know that what he did can never be forgiven unless he asks *Mechilla* from the other person." I harbored a secret to which only two other people knew about and no one could do nothing about it. I was fearful that this man would never understand me or my intention to help him stand before *Hashem* on *Yom Kippur*. I was fearful of his temper and of being humiliated by him myself.

I entered shul for *Mincha* on *Erev Yom Kippur*. I shuddered when the banker approached and stood right in front of me. I had never expected to see him. I had to decide whether or not to approach him. I struggled with the question all throughout the *Tefila*. I realized that I had no choice, and after *Mincha* I approached him in the lobby.

"Mr. Korn, can I speak to you for a moment?"

He stepped aside and we found a corner. My heart was pounding. I had never felt so exposed and vulnerable before in my life.

"Mr. Korn, it's *Erev Yom Kippur* and I know that tomorrow you'll do *Tshuvah* with great sincerity. But there is something that I need to share with you. You see, I was a witness a few months ago when you argued with Mr. Slotkin. You tore into him in a way that I have never witnessed before, and don't think I will ever see again. I don't need to know what happened after and whether you and he ever spoke again. In the event that you haven't spoken, you may want to consider some contact with him before *Yom Hadin*."

He looked at me with incredulity. I couldn't decipher the reaction. He turned red and simply said: "I hear you."

I waited for the blast, but it never came. He left for home and so did I.

The next morning, *Yom Kippur* morning, I was walking into shul. I saw him. He said nothing to me. That afternoon, as I took a short walk during the break, he approached me.

"I owe you a debt of gratitude. I called Mr. Slotkin before *Yom Tov* and apologized. I never would have done it without your help. Thank you." He had a tear in his eye. We were both aware of it. To this day, Mr. Korn and I share a special relationship of mutual respect.

I think of this incident because I can't remember being in a more vulnerable situation. He could have cut me up, as he did earlier to another person. Instead it led to many positive developments and a special relationship. Vulnerability means giving up control, risking and taking a chance. More important, it becomes a bond between two people seeking a relationship.

What does this mean in marriage? Vulnerability means being able to say: "I was wrong and I'm sorry." It means admitting that positions which were forcefully defended may now be seen as incorrect and you need to climb back from the limb. What will your husband or wife say when you admit you were wrong? Will your vulnerability be protected and safeguarded?

Vulnerability is the key to the next gate. If you have proceeded to the point where you are interested in another person, now is the time to see whether this person is able to protect you when you demonstrate vulnerability. It's the equivalent to putting yourself in an emotional wind tunnel. Only your wings are not being tested. You are testing your partner's ability to hear, respond to and respect your vulnerability.

Michael had struggled with a weight problem for many years. He and Carol had been dating for months with little progress. Neither was sure of whether they wanted to proceed. Both were aware of the weight problem yet it was a taboo issue. Michael had called me about whether he wanted to proceed. He was unsure whether he had any deep feelings for her. I asked him whether they had ever discussed his weight problem. They hadn't. I suggested that he test out just how well she accepted his vulnerability around the weight issue. I asked him to tell her that he wanted to discuss a personal challenge he had been struggling with and to bring up the weight issue. Then, after casting his jewel into the pond, wait to see her response.

He called me back a few days later. Her response surprised him. She said that of course she knew he had this problem and trusted that he was trying to do something about it. But she always wondered whether he was courageous enough to discuss it with her. Now that he has brought it up, she feels a deeper sense of respect for his honesty and openness. She was sure that together they would find a way of helping him. He literally melted from a sense of relief. He now trusted her to protect him.

It became a deciding moment in helping him move forward toward marriage. In all of his dreams and fantasies he could never have predicted such a response.

VII. SEVEN GATES TO THE KINGDOM OF MARRIAGE

It opened up a wellspring of feelings and affection for her. He understood at that moment that for the first time since they had started dating he could see himself marrying her. A few weeks later they were engaged.

Sometimes vulnerability is sharing your own commitments and conflicts as a single with a lifestyle which is so important to your balance and emotional survival. It may very well be all you have and regardless of who the person is you are dating, you may be very fearful of giving it up. Therefore, what would happen if you would tell your date:

"There's something I want to share with you. We've been dating for a few months and I really feel comfortable with you. I've even thought about marriage. However, the more I think about marriage, the more I start to think about what it would do to my life. How it would affect my job, my relationship with my friends, my habits. Do you ever think about these things yourself?"

This question will help you understand more about this person's ability to accept and appreciate the complexities of being human and undergo the enormous change involved in marriage.

Vulnerabilities also don't have to be specific to fears about marriage. They can also be related to other issues, especially related to apologies for even minor infractions. These become extremely important in showing honesty and a willingness to bend.

Shulamis and Benjy had very different styles of communicating. He was more intellectual and she more feeling oriented. Shulamis always assumed that Benjy was "holding back" his feelings. Yet Benjy was clearly the more intellectual type and resented Shulamis's assumptions that he was holding back emotionally. I spoke to Shulamis and suggested that she use this as a way of showing vulnerability. On the next date, she said: "Benjy, I owe you an apology. I really have to live with the fact that we are not clones of each other and that you have a more intellectual approach to life than I do."

Benjy couldn't believe his ears. He immediately told her how important it was for him to hear her say this. He also showed his great concern over not feeling that he was right and she wrong. It was his concern for her vulnerability that really spoke to her and brought them closer together.

Sometimes vulnerability requires a reassessment of whom we are and in turn leads others to assess who they are. Hillel had his first date with Shulie. He was concerned because Shulie had been raised in a more Zionist-oriented home than the yeshiva type environment he had grown up in. Their first two dates went according to plan. Hillel wanted to go further. I suggested that he admit to Shulie that he had stereotyped her as being too Zionist and wanted to apologize for stereotyping her without looking deeper into the person. At first he balked. He felt it was demeaning to him and putting her on the spot. I insisted and he gave in. The result was that on hearing his "apology" she said: "I've been harboring serious doubts about your ability to respect and trust me that I have become serious about my *Yiddishkeit*. Now that you have said this, I feel I can respect you, trust you and even consider assuming *Minhagim* which you feel closer to."

VII. SEVEN GATES TO THE KINGDOM OF MARRIAGE

❦ *Preparing Your Human Vulnerabilities*

If you can't find your car in the parking lot after a date and you apologize profusely, you have not expressed human vulnerability. Your vulnerability is your admission that you have a flaw, a weakness, an imperfection which you understand and are attempting to bring under control. If this flaw impacts on your dating partner, it makes it even more effective to determine what the ripples will be.

So ask yourself:
Was I insensitive to this person during our dates?
Do I have a personal problem that I'm working on that I want to reveal?
Did I say or do something on our dates for which I want to apologize?

❦ *Jewels For the Pond*

Once you have decided on an appropriate area, wait for the right moment, when you will not be interrupted and drop your jewel in the pond. Now stand back and watch the ripples.

≑ *Human Vulnerability — In Conclusion*

If you have opened yourself up by exposing your vulnerability and have received a response which is reassuring, then you know that you have found a rare person. There is no better indication of the promise a relationship holds for two people than the experience of: "I have shown you that I can be vulnerable and you have responded by protecting me and being considerate of my weakness. Therefore I feel a sense of gratitude and closeness to you." If this can occur, then you are indeed very close to the relationship which far exceeds your most prized fantasies.

The Gate of Caring

The Talmud tells us that the Torah begins and ends with *chesed*- kindness. Caring is at the core of all lasting relationships.

With the help of your Inner Circle you have moved through the first four gates of the relationship. These first gates helped define the qualities of the person you are dating. You were able to determine by the "ripples" created on their behavior that the relationship has promise. By now you should be ready to seriously consider whether marriage is a potential reality or just a distant and unrealistic dream. Your first step toward a determined and focused drive toward marriage is through caring. Through this gate of caring you are demonstrating that you have the capacity to offer a level of chesed and kindness that a loving marriage requires.

Caring is beyond affirmation or human vulnerability. In affirmation you have selected personal Midos to admire as a way of telling a person that you value their goals and direction in life. In human vulnerability you have offered admission of a weakness to determine that your dating partner will not exploit your weaknesses and will express their ability to be protective and considerate. In Caring your jewel is based on a principle which governs all human existence and behavior. It is that *Hashem* has created each of us to struggle with life's challenges. The very nature of our lives is to grow through challenges and adversity. No one, whether we are tall, short, younger, older, wealthy or financially limited, escapes life's challenges. We all walk a tightrope.

A few years ago I had the occasion to enter the office of one of the wealthiest men in America. The office was beyond question the most lavishly appointed, massive and impressive corporate setting I had ever seen. I was literally mesmerized. Aside from being the CEO of a number of large corporations, he was also an art collector. The office was filled with rare art works. At his side was a model of his personal corporate jet. While I was waiting for him he was completing a phone conversation to purchase a major league ball team and its stadium. He got off the phone and we spoke for about 20 minutes. He then picked up a ton of files, stuffed them in his briefcase, under his arm and everywhere else he could find and started to walk out the door to fly off somewhere. He turned to me and said something to the effect: "Don't let the trappings of success fool you. My life is now ruled by this." He meant the files. He was telling me that he had become a victim of his own success. I was jarred from my initial impression of awe. I realized that he was *Bosor v'dom*- flesh and blood. I struggled with my challenges and sought answers and relief. He struggled with his challenges and sought answers and relief.

Why is this scene important to remember? Because people who date should always realize that everyone on this earth, including the two of you who are dating, are all walking a personal tightrope, attempting to maintain emotional and social balance and equilibrium in countless areas of life. Regardless of how comfortable, handsome, pretty, slim, or powerful, *Hashem* has placed us squarely within a life of personal challenges. It's the way we grow.

VII. Seven Gates To The Kingdom Of Marriage

Chazal says: *Mefum tzora agra* — from adversity we grow. This gate of Caring is reached after you have been out a number of times and have succeeded in moving beyond the first four gates. You now understand your partner's life struggles and achievements. Caring focuses on your ability to say to your dating partner: I understand and appreciate your struggles in life. In my understanding I have come to care for and respect you. And I want you to understand my caring as a gesture of my ability to and desire to be devotedly attached to you for life. Caring says: "I'm big enough to understand and encompass your struggles. That's why I can say that I am ready to marry you." Of course you're not proposing this very moment. But if your caring statement is felt and accepted as a gesture which hits the mark, then you have crossed a major threshold toward your goal of marriage.

Esther was 35 when she was dating Yosef. The couple had seen each other for three or four pleasant dates. There was a mutual sense of comfort. Yet they were stuck and unable to go any further. It's a feeling that many singles have after a few dates. You just run out of things to say, places to go. The dates started off pleasantly with a future filled with the promise of leading toward marriage. Suddenly, you run out of steam. You can't seem to cross over that hurdle which tells you: "This is the person I have been looking for all these years." This is where dates peter our and relationships grow stale and uninteresting. Remember. For a mature single to say, "I'm ready to marry," means they are ready to turn their entire life upside down for you. Everything they have built for themselves as a single has to be dismantled. So you have to be very sure that this is the right person. There is no way to survive a mistake at this stage of the game.

Esther sensed they were in trouble and called me to see if there was a way of going further and somehow deepening the bond.

"Tell me about him," I said.

"He's a computer analyst, lives in Brooklyn with his father, very pleasant, nice personality and just nice to be with." she answered.

"Any siblings?" I asked.

"I know of a sister, and I was told he has a twin brother, but he never mentions him."

I told her that if he had a twin brother they must be very close. I suggested she ask about his twin brother, if in fact he has one.

She called me back two days later and said that he did in fact have a brother, who died in an auto accident a couple of years ago.

My response to her was that when a twin brother is lost, a part of him was probably lost as well. It's like losing an arm or half of yourself. It was clear to me that that his loss is probably very deep and painful and there must be a vacuum in his life.

I suggested that Esther raise the issue at the next date, ask him about the accident, the shock, the loss and how it has effected his life. Esther was shocked to hear me suggest this. She felt it was inappropriate for a couple at this stage of their dating to be exchanging feelings at this level.

My response to her was that if Yosef was going to feel there was a person in this world with whom he could spend the rest of his life, then it could only be someone to whom this empty part of him meant something. If she could not respond, then there was no sense in continuing the relationship. It would always remain on the superficial level and eventually atrophy and die.

Esther called me back a few days later with all the information. It was a very moving date, and even draining. She wasn't used to such "heavy" dates. I helped her craft a Caring statement which essentially told Yosef that she thought about his loss and had begun to understand what a profound impact it had on his life.

If Esther was unready to express this statement, Yosef was even less prepared to hear it. He was absolutely surprised to hear this expressed on a date. It showed him that someone could understand him and he was deeply moved. It led him to open up and share how he has lived with an emptiness inside since his brother passed away. It was as if by accepting her caring he was confirming to her the he had found a soul mate who deeply cared and understood. He accepted her gesture of caring. The relationship took wings. Within a few weeks they were engaged.

This is why caring is at the center of all relationships. Because we all need it, regardless of whom we are. Whether we are rich or poor, successful or struggling, each of us is delicately balanced on the tightrope of life. This is our human condition which Hashem imbued us with. It's also the reason why we have to turn to each other. Caring about a person's life, their challenges, their triumphs in the face of adversity and accepting their weaknesses as part of being human, is the single most significant thing we can do to show we are serious about spending our lives together.

Caring is a powerful tool when it's based on what you have learned about a person through the gates of your relationship. It's a profound gift of human communication combining insight, understanding, empathy and an abiding respect for the life of the person you are dating. It says: "I'm watching you, hearing you, paying attention to you. I've put it all together and have arrived at the conclusion that you and your life mean something to me. I don't have simple answers. But I do understand and care very much about you and your life." It's not something you can fake. Because... you can't care unless you understand and you can't understand unless you care to understand. And when you do understand and care and have the courage and subtlety to express it, then you have scaled an emotional Everest, sailed an ocean separating two souls, won over a heart that had once been distant and inaccessible. You are very much on the road to marriage.

⸙ *Preparing Your Jewels of Caring*

Your first step is to honestly ask yourself, "What is my greatest struggle in life? Is it my loneliness, my conflict with my need to care for aging parents, my need to work hard, my insecurity about my possessions?" There is no need to be critical. Respect your struggle. It's the accumulation of years of living alone. Now that you have some better understanding of your own struggle, use it to understand the tightrope your dating partner walks. Ask yourself: "What do I understand about this person? What is his or her greatest challenge?" It could be a previous marriage which is still haunting. Perhaps it's loneliness, a loss of a loved one, a demanding job, a fear of change, or any other issue which plays a central role.

Your task is to first articulate it to yourself and then to your partner. Here is a scenario which touches on some of the potential issues. "We've been going out for some time and I believe it's very important that I understand what you have been expressing about yourself. Would you mind if I shared my impressions with you?

I'm sure that in some areas I'm off base and I appreciate hearing what you really mean. I have the impression that you're very committed to those things that are a part of your life, such as your students, your learning and caring for your parents. You've built your life around these areas. At the same time I sense that you are also seriously committed to the idea of marriage and building a family. You also want to be very sure that the person you marry will respect your commitments."

Here is another scenario. "I understand that losing your wife four years ago was a terrible loss and that you still feel her absence. You want to be sure that the woman you marry will be able to fill her loss and also be sensitive to the needs of your three young children."

Another scenario may go like this.

"Living these years as a single woman has given you a sense of healthy independence and self sufficiency, which you value. At the same time I sense that you very much want to marry. But the man you are looking for has to respect what you have built with your life and he must understand that before you agree to marry and change your life, you need to deeply feel trust and respect for him.

✥ Caring — In Conclusion

If you have grasped the meaning of caring, if you have understood that central issue in the life of your dating partner and if you have expressed your ability to care, then engagement and marriage is very much a reality which can occur with this person.

You have made it occur until now and you can make the rest happen. This is what creates a marriage.

VI. The Gate of Transformation - From "I" To "We"

The next gate in your relationship toward marriage is in changing how you see yourself. I call this the transformation from "I" to "We."

⚭ Becoming "We": From The Outside To The Inside

The first critical element necessary to experience this sense of being a part of another life is through the support, feedback and "cheering on" you receive from friends and others close to you. In my experience with dating couples, the single greatest influence which creates this transformation comes from the outside. It's when a couple consciously decides to "show" themselves to others as a couple, which gives others an opportunity to provide reinforcement, *Chizuk* (support) and validation. When a couple begins to see and hear others relate to them as a couple, it changes their sense of "who I am." The philosopher Decartes said "I think, therefore I am." For our couple it is, "We are seen as a couple, therefore we are."

But there is an obstacle to be overcome. Many singles feel uncomfortable about making the commitment to visit parents and even friends until there is a certainty about the future of the relationship. It feels too premature and too much of a commitment. They aren't yet convinced that this really is their *bashert*. Appearing before friends and relatives may solidify a relationship which is not ready to be solidified. They opt to wait until some kind of epiphany sends them through the ceiling with ecstatic certainty that there can not possibly be any other. Only then will they agree to be seen and hosted as a couple.

The secret to overcoming this dilemma is to distinguish between those people who can be trusted to understand the tentativeness of the relationship and the risk involved and those who will view your being together as a statement which is irrevocable. So the challenge of this gate is to spend time together with others who are valued and trusted: teachers, friends, family (providing they are helpful). Each meeting, meal, evening spent together provides more external reinforcement until you experience the transformation from "I" to "We." It is through these safe meetings with others that you begin to hear the silent message "We see you as a couple, as future man and wife and we share in your desire to build a life together."

Paul and Lisa had gone through 2 years of a stop-and-start relationship. They had gone out on perhaps twenty to thirty dates during this period and had been close to engagement two or three times. Paul was a doctor and Lisa an occupational therapist. Each time there was hope and each time it died. Over and over they said good-bye, thinking it was finished. Then, once again they were drawn together, unable to let go forever. Perhaps this time, they hoped, they could see it through to marriage.

I was called by Paul this "last and final" attempt. He was so sure it would happen and so was she. But history was repeating itself. They were ready to say good-bye once again. I spoke to Paul, learned of their erratic past. He asked for my assistance. I told him I would try to help, but that we had to start at the beginning. He insisted that they knew each other too well and didn't want to start as if they were having their first date. He insisted there was nothing new to discover or say. They had been through all this many times before. Without any other option available to him he yielded and began from the beginning, at affirmations. At first they moved rapidly, all the way through caring. There were a few interesting zigzags, but, they progressed. Everything was in place. Yet, regardless of how close they were becoming, they were both stuck, unable to make the next move toward engagement. I realized that something had to occur to bring them beyond their paralysis. They were doing everything right, but something was holding them back.

Considering different possibilities, I suggested they try and spend a Shabbos away together, perhaps with a family they both knew. Lisa declined, feeling it would create too much pressure. Finally, Lisa suggested they go to Montreal, where she was helping run a *Kiruv Shabbaton*, assisting a former teacher from Israel. There would be plenty of action with lots of kids and many old friends from Israel who would participate. Lisa felt it would be a safe way to be together for a *Shabbos*, with plenty of distractions.

I had no idea what the outcome would be, whether

it would end once again, or proceed on to the next step. Paul called me on Sunday night after they had driven back from Montreal.

"You know Shaya, at first I found the *Shabbos* together to be very difficult. We both felt distant and uninvolved with each other. I was ready to walk away once and for all and with no second thoughts. Then something happened. There was one moment which I have to tell you about. It was after *Havdallah,* when there were a lot of kids coming over to Lisa to tell her how much they appreciated her participation. I was standing next to her and feeling for the first time rather good about being there with her. Many of her friends started coming over and talking to us as if we were a couple ready to marry. At first I backed off. Then something started to change inside myself. It dawned on me that for the first time in my life I started to think of myself as a "We." Somehow, for the first time I started to see myself and Lisa as a pair. It was totally unexpected. All this time I had been blaming her for holding back. I realized that I was guilty as well. I claimed that I wanted to marry, but I really thought of myself in the singular. The moment I experienced that "We" feeling, I knew I could now go on to the next step."

As he was telling me of his feeling, I realized what I had never understood before. The next stage in the relationship is when perception of self as an "I" is transformed to a "We." It has no precedent, no preparation. It comes, for the most part, not from within, but from without- from the influence and encouragement of others. The mind and heart grasps, as if by osmosis, the wishes and gestalt of others. You are no longer perceived as being alone. You are a part of two people- a couple. Perhaps it's only a wish and a fantasy on the part of others. But, when it occurs after a solid foundation has been set, then their perception and wishes to see you as part of another person take hold. When it happens too early in the relationship, it has no effect. It may even feel inappropriate and an intrusion into your life. But when all the emotional pieces are in place, then you have a way of accepting their wishes and fantasies.

This is what happened to Paul and Lisa. From that moment, Paul knew it would progress on to marriage, because in his mind and heart he was now a part of a couple and Lisa was the other part. He realized that what he had been blaming her for, was in reality the absence of a perception within himself. The perception occurred when others were able to transmit to him what his own mind, as a single for many years, was unable to come to on its own. After that moment, he was determined not to let her get away. He would do whatever it took. Within two weeks, he took her to the same hotel lobby in which they had started their dating some 2 years ago. This time he proposed.

☙ *Becoming "We."*
From The Inside To The Outside

Consider another aspect in the lives of Paul and Lisa. The reality of marriage to another person can never be a leap into an unknown abyss. Internalizing the chizuk and encouragement of others and beginning to think of yourself as a "We," is not enough. For a mature single to seriously be emotionally free to marry, a major "rewiring" effort has to take place. Paul and Lisa, as singles had far too many personal commitments and interests in their lives as individuals to blindly jump into each other's lives, or permit the other person to jump into theirs.

Every part of their individual lives represents an investment carefully created over time, carefully thought out and nurtured. Yes, it wasn't marriage. But, it worked! They, or you simply will not throw away that which was so important and carefully constructed to bring in another person unless the emotional, social, financial and psychological wires are reconnected to accommodate this new relationship. It's not an issue of being carried away emotionally with someone else to the point of blind love. Careful consideration has to be given to this move of a lifetime. This is why the transformation from "I" to "We" must also encompass another element. This is the internalization of a new idea: all of your most precious relationships and personal investments, both social and financial have to be restructured. They now have to accommodate this new relationship as being more important than all the rest.

How is this achieved? It's achieved when, after all the other pieces are in place you say to each other," You and I have gone this far and we both feel there is a strong possibility of marriage. Yet we both want to be sure. I suggest that we spend the next thirty days making a serious effort to see whether we've both found the right person. Let's talk every day, see each other as much as possible, behave as if we're both sure. If after this period we're ready, let's go ahead and get engaged. If not, it's a sign that it will never happen."

VII. Seven Gates To The Kingdom Of Marriage

This is what has to happen to undergo the emotional and perceptual transformation from being a person alone to being a couple. It's the long hours you spend with each other, the letters, e-mail messages, the long phone calls, witty and cute voice mails, the flowers, small gifts, greeting cards, long walks together, the time you spend together with friends and family. It's all of these and more.

I call this period "a letter of intent." It's an attempt to get closer and help a new relationship work. If you see it's not working, then it's non-binding and you discontinue. The suggested rules of this period are, for thirty (or more) days you:

*1. Speak, communicate or meet
   on an almost daily basis.
2. Visit as many family and friends together.
3. Do not date anyone else.
4. Be conscious of the reality that engagement may
   very well occur even before the end of this period.
5. Be prepared to end the relationship
   if it hasn't occurred.*

This approach then gives you the chance to get to know each other in depth and sets the groundwork for a transformation to occur from both within yourself and from the influence of others.

This period also means taking a proactive role by visualizing the change marriage will bring into your life. It's far more than a feeling that marriage can happen. It's an exercise in visualizing the rearrangement of the emotional architecture, furniture and social fabric of your life.

If you want to experience yourself as part of a pair, then you have to make room in your emotional life for this person. This means a willingness to consciously share your possessions, your friends, your living space, your savings and mostly, your precious time. It doesn't mean writing a check for half your liquid assets or throwing out your furniture, or giving up your valued friends. It does mean becoming increasingly comfortable and accustomed to start thinking and visualizing your life as being shared with another person. Here are a few examples:

Elliot was feeling increasingly certain about marriage to Shira. But there was something holding him back. They were going to move into his apartment which was certainly large enough for both. But, the more he thought about her taking over the apartment, changing the feel of something he had spent years putting together, the more uneasy he felt. He couldn't see her changing the furniture, the paintings, the feel of life as he had known it for many years. It presented a problem.

Charna was ready to accept Mark's proposal for marriage. But she felt that Mark was too tied down to old friends, many of whom were single and lived nearby. He wanted to spend a *Shabbos* together with Charna and his friends before they would announce their engagement. Charna had questions. She felt that Mark's friends were not really for the relationship and would undermine their future together. Mark felt a deep loyalty to his friends. He felt hurt that Charna was questioning his relationship with them and began to wonder whether she could respect his freedom to choose his own friends.

Carol was about to accept a proposal for marriage. She called me feeling upset. "I know I'm crazy, but how can I do this to my roommate?"

Aaron is not happy about being single. However, he loves his freedom and has planned no less than three skiing trips this winter. He admits that having to consider another person's schedule would cramp his style.

Not one of these conflicts are fabricated or even unreasonable. We dare not laugh at them or feel they are absurd. Singles have created lives for themselves which are their support systems to maintain sanity and equilibrium. They can not be expected to disconnect themselves from this lifestyle before a new one is in place. It's simply human nature. Just consider what it must be like for singles who have spent a lifetime accumulating resources, possessions, developing a lifestyle that works for them, spending many hours caring for aging parents, commitment to professional interests and on and on. How do these people begin to make room to say: "I'm ready to let someone into my life and to share all I have and am with this person."?

The first step is to acknowledge, understand and respect the powerful pull on yourself and other singles. The next step is to engage in conscious visualizations where you actually start making room in your busy and very valued lifestyle for another person. Later in this chapter we will provide you with a visualization which cuts to the heart of this dilemma.

When all the pieces are in place, at an unexpected and unrehearsed moment, a new perception of yourself begins to emerge. You see yourself as part of another person's life and personality. It's a slow and hesitant change. Over time, your new identity takes on greater reality. The process ends when in your minds and hearts you have become a couple — a *zug* (pair). The next logical step is marriage.

≋ Preparing for Transformation from "I" to "We"

For a mature single, the most important insight to guide you through this phase of transformation is not to expect to do it alone. You start by respecting the power of those loyalties and commitments you have created in your life as a single and understand that each of these commitments and loyalties has likely contributed to your stability and well being. So understand that the transformation takes time and a focused effort. Here are a few ways to make the change happen in yourself:

1. *Suggest to your dating partner that you want to spend a period of time where you exclusively date each other.*
2. *During this time you will visit each other's friends and family.*
3. *You will both maintain contacts on a daily basis.*
4. *After this period you will see whether you are ready to become engaged or to stop the relationship.*

≎ *Transformation — In Conclusion*

Once you have internalized your change from "I" to "We" and have found the support of friends and relatives to reinforce this transformation, you're ready to take the final step. Realize that from here on there is no longer a risk. Your relationship is based on solid ground, of two people who have seriously established a foundation for a lifetime.

VII. *The Gate of Engagement & Marriage*

You have gone through all the gates to the kingdom, except one, which is your ultimate goal. This is the treasured prize of all your dreams and endeavors. The last gate of engagement and marriage is, without question, the most challenging. It represents that single act of commitment which has been so difficult to achieve. What makes engagement so challenging is that the closer couples get to know each other, care for each other, feel connected to each other, this closeness also brings greater clarity about each others flaws and human frailties.

I was once the senior editor for a magazine, Mosaic. For months and months I could dream of nothing more than getting that first beautiful issue out, just as we had planned. Everything would be letter perfect, from the high end graphics to the well written stories. It was intended to be a quality magazine, designed for the privileged few who had contributed large donations to Jewish Federations. It was fashioned after Town and Country or Architectural Digest. A glossy publication with well crafted articles about Jewish art and culture. After exhausting months of editing, shoots, graphic design and printing it was finally finished. It was quite beautiful and impressive. The praise was wonderful to hear. However, I, as the senior editor, who knew every

VII. Seven Gates To The Kingdom Of Marriage

nook and cranny, every corrected typo, every shoot and re-shoot until it was all painstakingly put together, had a very different feeling than I had planned. I was proud of the praise, but also very well aware of the flaws, the deadlines, the battles over egos and sensitivities, the struggle to squeeze out each penny from advertising revenues. I learned that the closer we get to realizing a "dream," the more we scrutinize it. It's like looking at a TV screen up close. It's no longer a picture, just millions of pixels and dots.

It's the same when getting closer to people. In growing up, many kids have difficulties when their minds and perceptions mature. Until now, parents were strong and without human flaws. As they grow they begin to see their parents as human beings who struggle with many issues and sometimes decide on the wrong side. These kids get older, they see more, they see flaws. For singles, dating is geared to get each of you closer, as close as possible. Yet, when it's about to lead to engagement and you're as close as you're ever going to get, many singles begin to focus on the flaws. They panic and can't remember or perceive the beauty of the relationship and everything they've built together. They know too much. They get scared. They've invested so much of themselves and now it's unthinkable to back away. Panic is not unheard of before engagement. The bottom line is that it's unknown territory and requires a great leap.

I remember as a kid, approaching the edge of the high board. I had studied that diving board and the pool below it for some time, preparing myself for my great leap into self esteem. By now I was confident that I could take the leap from that unheard of height. I knew

I could swim and I could dive. I got the courage and jumped. On the way down I said to myself : "What did I do?????" For a few seconds I was free falling, facing an unknown fate and quite frightened. But I was already in motion and couldn't turn back. Then I hit the water. I made it. It was cold and delicious and was very much worth the effort.

It may very well be the same with engagement. Seeing the flaws up close represents the other side of all the good things that were focused on until now. The thought of engagement brings out the other side of the ambivalence. It's enough to drive many people away from taking that plunge, regardless of the time and effort invested in reaching this point in the relationship. I know of one young woman who has backed away from two separate engagements. On both occasions she was certain that her Chosson was the right person. On both occasions she panicked. It started off with small petty doubts and nit- picking. Then the doubts grew to giant proportions. As long as you haven't taken the leap and landed, the conflict and fear can easily get you focused on the flaws. It's only when you take the leap and land that everything changes. You suddenly understand that being engaged is a whole new way of living. It's a blissful and unaltered certainty and calmness. It's arriving.

Recently I received a call from a young man I was coaching. He had been preparing to ask this young woman to be his Kallah. He planned the date, the question, the staging, everything. But when it came time to ask his mind started racing. He was getting cold feet. He ran to a phone and called me:

"Shaya , I'm here together with Malkie. Now, I'm not

sure. I had it all planned out. But I got to thinking, maybe it's not so clear. I'm beginning to wonder about a lot of things. It's all coming at me so quickly."

"Okay Dovie, what's bothering you?"

"I'm looking at her. Suddenly she looks too thin. Then she looks too short. Then she speaks too quickly. Then she's not pretty enough. I ask whether she really knows me and whether I'm ready to spend the rest of my life with her. Shaya, I'm telling you, I can't handle it. I'm losing it. I think I'm going to call it off."

"Dovie, does Malkie have any idea about what's happening?"

"Not a clue."

"Why not? If I were you I'd say, 'Look Malkie. We got this far, but suddenly I'm feeling very edgy. I want to go further, but I'm stuck.' Do you understand what I mean?"

Dovie listened on the phone.

"You mean I can say that?"

A few hours passed. The phone rang.

"Shaya, Mazel Tov. I'm a Chosson."

'Mazel Tov! But what happened after I spoke to you'?

"Well I told her just what you suggested. She listened and then said. 'Dovie I understand that you have last minute questions. The fact is that I already made up my mind about you and want to go on. If you need more time, I can certainly handle that.' "

"Oh no!" Dovie said to himself, "what did I get myself into?"

Then he told me. "You know what I told her? I said: 'Well, Malkie actually I also made up my mind, I just got a bit frightened. It's a big move, you know?' Then I said to myself, "Oh no, what did I say now?????' "

"The next thing I knew we were engaged and calling everyone we knew."

Listening to Dovie I couldn't help thinking about diving off the high board. You get yourself as ready as possible, take the leap and then, when you've taken the leap and you're in mid-air, you say: "Oh no, what did I get myself into?" But is there any new experience in life that doesn't require this leap of faith that's based on sound and thoughtful preparation? At some moment real courage is required to go forward. And somewhere along the line you are going to be in very strange and uncharted territory.

After the dive, the beauty is in hitting the water. Then you feel the comforting envelopment of that cold reassuring liquid all around you. There is pure pleasure, free of doubts and conflict. Suddenly all seems so absolutely good, pure, right and perfect. But it's only momentary. Sooner or later you have to come out of that pool and on to dry land. With engagement, the experience just begins.

I have a close friend who, when younger, was about to become engaged. Suddenly he was frightened. He ran to a phone and called his *rosh yeshivah* to ask him what to do. He was told, "Why are you so scared? Do it. It will be the happiest period of you life." He listened to his *rosh yeshivah*. He will acknowledge today, years later, that it was the best piece of advice anyone ever gave him. Because when the engagement comes, so does the most remarkable personal transformation that you will ever experience. Suddenly all the flaws, all the fears, all the hesitation disappears. Like magic they vanish. In the place there is a serenity and even complacency.

I have watched with utter amazement how the

questions of yesterday no longer exist as they give way to a child-like innocence of two people suddenly together, on top of the world. Everything is roses, creating moments of exquisite security and certainty. This is when you understand that this is the best decision you have ever made. Somehow it all falls into place. I have often thought of this period like the period following childbirth. A mother struggles to give birth to a fetus which she has never seen. The birthing process is painful and filled with anxiety. But once the child comes into the world, there is only mother and child. The intimacy and closeness is unparalleled in any aspect of creation. It is the perfect human union. In a mother's eyes every child is beautiful. In the eyes of a chosson and kallah, they are the most wonderful and beautiful people in the world.

Chaim and Shaindy struggled for many months to finally reach their moment of engagement. Until now their relationship was filled with many questions and doubts. After working through the many issues and feeling the support of friends and family, Chaim finally proposed and Shaindy accepted. Chaim was immediately overcome with a feeling of absolute love and commitment for Shaindy. It was as if a hidden side of him suddenly emerged. "Shaindy, I never realized before how beautiful you are." Was it her beauty, or was it like the mother who looks at her new born with unquestioned love and beauty? It's a stage of human relationships which *Hashem* has prepared for us all. First at birth, then at engagement and marriage. And with this stage he placed a desire and ability in our eyes to see nothing but absolute love and beauty.

≋ When You Must Initiate Engagement, Use Butterflies

If you feel you are waiting for your dating partner to initiate the "E" issue and you want to get things moving without seeming too pushy, you can use a gentle yet effective method. Tell your dating partner that you have been giving the relationship much thought and feel it has a lot of promise. For that matter you have actually made up your mind. But, you admit, you do have some butterflies in your stomach. This will enable your partner to understand where you are and permit him or herself to acknowledge that it's quite natural to be somewhat anxious.

Another method, which is a bit more bold is to repeat the opening of the "butterflies" approach and then say, "I'm ready. But if you need more time, that's okay with me."

≋ Preparing for Engagement

Engagement is the dream that may have seemed impossible. I remember expecting our first child. It seemed like an impossibility. There was no precedent. The difference, of course, was that the process was biological and occurring within my wife. I had to do nothing, but perhaps say a few *Kapitalach Tehillim*. With engagement it is so much different. But the dream is just as impossible. Nothing can happen on its own. You have to set it in motion, plant the seeds and move forward. At this stage, after you have gone through so many precious moments, there is no reason to walk on eggshells. A woman need not wait patiently for the man. Men are far more reticent to make the commitment.

1. *Close your eyes.*

2. *Imagine yourself in a dark field illuminated by a warm fire nearby.*

3. *You can see this courageous person from your Inner Circle emerging from the darkness illuminated.*

4. *This person sits down next to you and says: "You too are a person of inner strength and courage. You realize that this may be a difficult and challenging moment for you. However, you also realize that such an opportunity is given to you once in a lifetime. So take a deep breath, feel your strength and resolve and step forward to make the most important commitment you will ever make to another human being."*

5. *And as this person finishes, another figure emerges from the darkness into the illuminating light of the flame.*

6. *This person sits down beside you and you hear yourself say: "I am ready to commit myself to you in marriage. I am ready to make a commitment to you for the rest of my life."*

7. *Take a deep breath. Know that you have the ability to show great personal strength and courage for the person you have been searching for these many years.*

⚜ Interactive Exercises

Use the visualization in the Gate of Hope which describes the wedding ceremony, family and home to internalize your feeling of engagement.

Speak to those who influence your partner to ensure that he or she is getting the message that it's time to make the jump

⚜ Jewels For The Pond

For this one, there is only one jewel. It's a diamond. And it doesn't go into the pond. It fits on a finger.

VIII. The Dating Experience

*N*ow that you have prepared for each of the seven gates to marriage, we can begin a practical step by step approach to dating, using the insights you've gained in the visualizations, interactive exercises and the jewels you will cast into the pond. This section has been prepared for you to follow, step by step, as you move toward marriage.

1. Taking Control

The key to success is simply to take control of your dating experiences and never let go. Not for a moment. You achieve this through your clear focus. I recently received a call from a friend about a single man in his thirties, Yisroel. Yisroel had been calling my friend and pressing him to arrange dates. His only request was that she should "be pretty." Sounds like a reasonable request. The problem was that Yisroel had been out with perhaps two hundred girls. He was the one to determine who was "pretty." It reminds me of a fellow who puts down $50,000 for a Lexus. He feels great, on top of the world. Then he sees a scratch. His balloon bursts. He feels, angry and cheated. Suddenly his life is turned upside down. The same with Yisroel. He's looking for his idea of physical perfection. He'll never find it. *Hashem* didn't create us that way. We see beauty and wholeness only when we feel wholeness inside. Clearly, the next date wouldn't be any different than the first two hundred. Yisroel may have potential, but he has little access to his potential. He's too confused about real priorities in life. He reminds me of a gunslinger in the old western movies, as I say to myself, "Whoever goes out with Yisroel next has to be in control. Otherwise he'll shoot down another one."

The key to success in dating is in controlling the process from beginning to end. Starting from the questions you ask the Shadchon, to what you say during the first phone call and on to dating. When one partner is focused and controls the process there is a real chance of things happening. Until now, Yisroel controlled things. He won by losing perhaps ten years of his life in which he could have been married. Now it was time to take control away from him and maybe, just maybe, give him a chance to get married.

So, from beginning to end, we will walk you through the dating process, with you in control.

2. It's Best To Have A Mentor.

To use this program it's best to have a friend, family member, rabbi, rebbetzin, someone with whom you can talk and share your progress and questions. As you move forward you will need the benefit of advice and input from this trusted third party, able to help you read developments and encourage you to move forward. Don't think you can do it alone. No one can. Get used to the idea that you need assistance and select that person who you can trust.

3. Prepare Your Inner Circle

Next, you need an experiential wellspring which feeds your focus and guides you, keeping you far away from the inane superficialities that pervade dating. You will achieve this through your Inner Circle and your focus on hope and belief that your life can change very quickly. The real difference between success and failure in this program is in selecting the moments and memories associated with your Inner Circle. These memories will give you the stability and emotional depth you need to move forward. It's best to write them down using a format like this:

Inner Circle	**Memory**	**Experience**
Rabbi	Meeting in his house	Trust and confidence
Grandmother	Receiving gift	Cared for and valued
Father	Bar Mitzvah embrace	Love & accomplishment

Once you've defined your Inner Circle, start to

cultivate these memories whenever you have the chance. Using these as anchors on dates will give you a wonderful resource upon which you can always draw.

4. Learn How To Cast Your Jewels In The Pond

Learn how to be a skilled dating partner. Remember, you are casting your jewels into a pond of your date's life and personality. Each jewel has two roles. The first is to make a personal and meaningful connection. The second role is to help you determine whether your date possesses the qualities you are focused on at each level. Your goal is to observe changes in facial qualities, verbal exchanges and other important indicators of how your date is responding. Your progress is dependent on your ability to read and feel the ripples. They tell the story of an emerging relationship.

5. Avoid the Superficial Search for "Perfection"

If you're like Yisroel, looking for short, tall, pretty, thin, svelte and all these other superficial signs of your *bashert*, it's a sure sign that you are either shallow or hopeless. Any hope or desire for the perfect date is the invention of hopelessness and defeat. On the other hand, if you are focused on the Midos side, which looks at your date's ability to give, to be open, caring, genuine and reflective, then you have a real chance of moving forward.

These qualities are not worn on anyone's sleeve. They must be tapped and revealed. You role is to give your date the opportunity to reveal this side of themselves. Think of dating as a pleasant attempt of two people starting a journey together. The difference is that you will be guided through each of the seven gates by a clear focus of your goals, as well as the emotional anchors provided by your Inner Circle. Even if you are sure that the person you are dating is not for you, stay with the relationship as long as you can move through each of the gates. Relationships which lead to marriage are based on feelings and experiences which you could have never planned or thought possible. With each gate your perception changes. What you thought as an impossible Shidduch may very well turn out to be the person that Hashem brought into the world to be your bashert and vice versa.

6. *Start Your Research.*

Calling a date is not a cold call. And if you are waiting for an initial call, you want to be just as prepared. Remember, the key to dating is that someone has to know where you are headed. If there are two people who are lost, the situation is bound to fail. Once you know who your date is you need to collect the following data, which you will use in your statements of hope, affirmations, inner history and caring:

1. Approximate age

2. Profession

3. Interests and hobbies

4. Affiliations with shuls, organizations

5. Family status (parents, siblings, previous marital and family history)

6. Personal preferences and lifestyle issues

7. Level of religious commitment, Israel, etc.

8. Friends and acquaintances

9. Milestone events which have impacted on this person's life

7. Start Calling

You can now get started. Here are a few points to remember:

- *You are learning to take control of the dating process.*
- *You are starting a relationship strengthened and directed by your Inner Circle.*
- *You no longer have to look for the perfect date.*
- *You are out to create relationships with everyone you date.*

And one of these relationships will be your bashert.

Start by asking for help from your friends, relatives and colleagues. They may very well have given up trying to help you because of past attempts or the feeling that you are no longer interested. Reawaken the interest on their part by saying, "I would really appreciate you helping me find a date. It doesn't have to be perfect or even close to perfect. Here are my general criteria. Even an impulse idea is fine. I trust in your instinct to come up with some creative ideas."

This will free them up to start thinking freely and creatively about whom they know for you. I know of so many shidduchim which began when someone suddenly thought of a person so obviously matched. Yet it took a moment of creative insight to see what was in front of them all along.

Recently a friend, who is a teacher, was trying to find a shidduch for her daughter. She was spending endless hours thinking of who she could call to locate young men. One day in the school hallway a fellow teacher came over and said: "I know you're looking high and low for a shidduch for your daughter. Didn't you ever consider Moshe?" Moshe happened to be a teacher in the school as well and she had known him for almost 3 years. For some reason the idea never hit her. The end of the story? They dated and married. So get others to start thinking about you again. Sooner or later something will click.

8. Start Remembering Previous Dates

Dating will never be the same. And if you had the chance to date all over again, each of your dates would now be a different story. For all you know, you may have already dated your bashert and not known it. I have a close friend who dated literally hundreds of young women. He went out with one after the other, never finding what he was looking for. After endless years and the onset of desperation, he started constructing a list of every young woman he went out with. He said to himself: "Some time over these years I must have gone out with someone who could be my wife." He selected a few candidates with whom he could go out with once again. The very first date turned out to be his wife.

He was unrealistic, rigid and impersonal. When he loosened up he discovered that the treasure had already been in his hands and he let it slip away. You can't recognize your *bashert* when you're unrealistic. You can only recognize this person by going through stages of a relationship where you are both undergoing subtle changes and observing the ripples.

I know very well that you've looked over your previous dates and can't find anyone. But that's the old you, the helpless you. Now you're running the show, clear about your approach, and things will be very different. When you start creating changes in your attitude you also create changes in perception. For example, Miriam was waiting for Chaim to propose. She was very nervous and tense. But the more Chaim sensed pressure, the more he went into a shell and moved away. Chaim's anxiety was fusing with Miriam's feeling of inner tension. Suddenly Chaim saw too many problems. He was stricken with fears that she was too connected to her family, too talkative, too controlling. Everything hit him at once. I encouraged Miriam to back off and relax. Almost immediately Chaim started to feel comfortable again and saw marriage as a real possibility.

It's the same person. A changed attitude leads to a change in perception. Start looking at your former dates with a new feeling of competence and mastery over how you will be "running the show."

You may have seen your *bashert* many years ago. But neither of you had set up the rules. You may have been both standing next to each other in Grand Central Station, each one thinking the other broke the appointment. The problem was that, like Miriam's anxiety, you were Chaim and at that moment thought your bashert just never arrived.

It's time to get out the pencil and start getting a list together of all the people you have ever dated. Next to each write what you liked and what you disliked. Attempt to note as many as possible that you would consider going out with again. Once you have one or more candidates, start calling to find out if this person is still available and then inquire if there is still an interest. The best way to begin is through someone who will make the initial contact for you and will stay involved until the relationship is strong and moving forward.

9. Get a Shadchon to Restart the Engine

If you have someone with whom there is "unfinished business," get a Shadchon who will contact this person. If your instincts tell you that this former date may reject you because of past performance, whatever may have happened, one way to get things started again is through a letter. Through the Shadchon ask for permission to send a letter.

This sample note will give you a flavor of what could be helpful in laying down an understanding for the relationship.

Dear _____

It has been _____ since you and I have seen each other. I'm sure that, as in my own life, many things have transpired in your life as well. As we go through different experiences we also come to see and feel things differently. Perhaps that's why I thought of you after all this time and asked myself whether at this stage in our lives it may make sense to see each other again. Of course, neither you nor I can make any commitments, but I can assure you that, if you agree to see me, I will approach a relationship with all the serious intention it deserves. You can respond to _____ who has already graciously agreed to serve as a contact person between us.

I hope you will give serious consideration to my request and look forward to speaking with you.

Best Wishes ...

10. The Phone Call — Your First Opportunity to Take Control

You've made contact. Your date is ready to hear from you or will be contacting you first. A phone call is arranged. This is your opportunity to seize the moment and start taking control. Don't let a breath go by without establishing your ability to steer this ship to port as quickly and successfully as possible.

Your goal in this first phone call is to assume control by creating an unexpected change in perception. Carefully use your Inner Circle and initial affirmations. It's important to remember that your date has information and ideas about you. Perhaps they've seen a picture of you or know someone who has already dated you. Preconceived perceptions or images are always harmful because it means you have to break through a stereotype, positive and negative, which is never you and in no way resembles you. To move the date forward on to a level playing field you have to break the stereotype and let them understand that their image of you is inadequate and has to be reconsidered.

Here are the rules for the first phone call. Follow them carefully and don't yield an inch.

A. Before you call, prepare 2 or 3 low level affirmations which you have learned from your contacts, sources, and Shadchon. These affirmations should deal with the person who is arranging the date, your date's profession, or any other piece of information which can be used for this initial affirmation. Write these affirmations down and keep them in front of you.

B. Get yourself in focus and remember your Inner Circle and your images of hope and belief. Once you have decided which experience from your Inner Circle you want to focus on, write it down and place it where you can read it while on the phone.

C. During the initial call, keep the call as pleasant and brief as possible while sharing your affirmations. Don't stay on too long. It may make you feel good, but may only detract from your chances of getting a serious relationship going. The longer you talk the greater the chance of creating more misconceptions and unrealistic expectations. Singles can feel secure and protected by the phone and stay on for as long as possible, harboring fantasies about someone's appearance while trying to sound witty, interesting and very special. The first call may last thirty minutes. But when the couple meets, there is no way to compete with each other's fantasies. You have essentially set yourself up to fall far short of the other's expectations.

D. Aside from the affirmations, be practical, set up a time and place for the date and then say good-bye. Don't waste an important affirmation for the phone call. You will not be able to judge the response or reaction, either on the person or on yourself. You should end the call with a statement of optimism and hope.

The phone call should be something like this:

> *"Hi, this is Chaim Sanders. I was told by Mrs. Bloom that you would be expecting my call."*
> *Pause and wait for response.*
> *(Affirmation): "I appreciate your willingness to get together. I must tell you that you certainly have a friend in Mrs. Bloom. She speaks the world of you. You certainly know how to choose friends."*
> *Pause and wait for response.*
> *"Is there any place special you would like to go?"*
> *"What time is convenient?"*
> *"How should we arrange a meeting place that's convenient?"*

(Affirmation): "By the way, I must say, *Rebbetzin* Bloom told me
that you attend her lectures. She certainly is a powerful speaker and a dedicated teacher."
Wait for response.
(Hope) "Then I'll look forward to seeing you on........"

11. Progressing Through The 7 Gates

The pieces are in place. The pace of progress through the seven gates is determined solely by your comfort level. These levels are not to be understood as seven gates equals seven dates. The intention is for you to cast your "jewels in the pond" and determine whether you are ready to move to the next gate. You may want to think over the "ripples" for a few hours or days, or even weeks. You may even travel through a number of gates in a single evening. It's a function of comfort level and your ability to assimilate a very intense and focused experience in interpersonal relationships.

☙ *Golden Rule*

Before you begin to date, make a commitment to yourself that you will proceed through the first four gates regardless of your initial feelings about your date. These initial stages will give an impression that you are a genuinely considerate person, but will not mislead anyone to feel you are considering marriage. Without the feedback from these stages you will have no basis to determine who your dating partner really is. The qualities that these gates will elicit will give you a chance to see the real person. Without them, your are simply looking at a unidimensional figure who may or may not be your *bashert*. You have no foundation to make any initial decision and all you are doing is continuing the cycle of missed opportunities.

♔ *The 1st Gate: Hope*

Because your focus on hope and belief are so critical, your first task is to sit down and work on your inner feelings of hope and optimism. There is a *halacha* that when a person steps into a *shul* to *daven*, first pause for a few moments and acquire a focus and a perspective. This is because we wear the burdens and the tempo of the outside world. Before we speak to *Hashem* we need to pause, catch our emotional and sometimes physical breath before we have the perspective to *daven*. Singles who are older carry their battle scars deeply embedded in their hearts and minds. Focus carefully on your images and feelings of hope.

> 1. *Find a quiet place and use the visualizations for hope and belief.*
> 2. *Be certain that you feel confident in your eventual success - G-D willing.*
> 3. *Focus on your Inner Circle experience.*
> 4. *Make your first calls and contacts until you begin to get results.*

VIII. THE DATING EXPERIENCE

✤ *The 2nd Gate: Affirmations for the First Date*

Make sure your date is planned as thoroughly a possible, particularly your affirmations. They should be based on issues that you truly value and admire, but not too personal or intimate so as to embarrass or put anyone on the spot. Select those issues about your date's values and dedications in life which you actually admire. For the initial phone call select milder affirmations such as choice of friends, a rabbi, a hobby, etc. Remember, this initial affirmation for the phone is to establish control over the process, not to make any deep connections. Phone conversations are one dimensional. Never waste a great affirmation on a phone call. You can't make the necessary eye contact, see the gestures and responses. It's all wasted on the phone.

Before the first date be careful about planning the following:

> 1. *Choose your Inner Circle experience and focus on it.*
>
> 2. *Select a mentor or a friend with whom you will review your date preparations and your evaluations after the date.*
>
> 3. *Arrange your date to be in a place where you can talk in privacy.*
>
> 4. *Don't spend too much money on food and drink . It creates a distraction as you add up*

the dollars and try to be on your best behavior because of the ambiance of an expensive restaurant.

5. *Make sure you're both in an area with room to walk around and sufficient distractions to reduce self consciousness. Ideal places include the botanical garden, museum, zoo, hotel lobby, etc.*

6. *Plan the affirmations you will discuss based on what you know about your date*

7. *Plan to make at least two or more affirmations. You plan by first writing them down, then rehearsing them and finally bringing the paper with you on the date. Otherwise you will probably forget to say them.*

8. *Space the affirmations apart.*

9. *After each affirmation, wait to see and hear the ripples you have created.*

10. *Get yourself focused on your Inner Circle and feelings of hope.*

11. *After the date is over, regardless of your initial feelings of either elation, pessimism or even neutrality, give the date a few hours and even over night to settle in. Many things happen on a date which have to be processed over time and discussed with other people who can help you sort out the issues.*

VIII. THE DATING EXPERIENCE

For the first date, you should prepare more serious affirmations:

> 1. *I admire the fact that as a teacher you can be so devoted to your student's development.*
>
> 2. *I think it's quite an achievement to attend daf Yomi on a daily basis for the full cycle.*
>
> 3. *I understand you're very close to the Stone family. It tells me that the people you admire are very Chashuv (important).*

≋ Assessment

1. Hold on to your focus on your Inner Circle experience to help you assess the relationship. In the same way that your Inner Circle has been giving and kind to you, that's how you should feel toward your date.

2. When you finish your date try to think through the following:

> • *How did this person respond to the affirmation (s)?*
> • *How did I feel about their responses?*
> • *Is this a person who can accept compliments and return them?*
> • *How comfortable did I feel with this person?*
> • *Is there anything which prevents me from trying to date this person again?*

Understand that first dates are only preliminary. Make every attempt to try for a second date.

❦ The 3rd Gate: The Inner History

Your next date will now take you to the dimension of your partner's life decisions. There are many things you may want to know in these areas. Asking these questions which touch at the heart of inner values, feelings and attitudes will provide you with a depth of understanding about this person. You need to get a feel for the inner person before you can continue to develop this relationship.

First select your memory of your Inner Circle which you will want to focus on. Now plan your questions. Here are a few examples:

- *You went to the Hebrew Academy. I know some people who went there. Tell me, who influenced you most when you went there?*
- *What made you decide to go into graphic design as a career? When did it first strike you that you wanted to make a career out of it?*
- *I heard you spent time living in Israel. What made you decide to go and live there?*
- *How did you find life to be when you were there?*
- *It must have been very difficult growing up without the support of a community. How did you manage to stay frum under those conditions?*
- *What was it like being in medical school,*

VIII. THE DATING EXPERIENCE

being away from your family for so long?

Remember to hold on to your focus as you ask questions and assess the answers. Once you have asked your questions be attentive as to what and how your questions are being answered. What are these answers telling you about the person, his or her personal values, inner strength determination, focus and drive? Do the answers suggest an inner reflectiveness, an openness, an insight into his or her lives? Do they fascinate interest or move you? Do they deepen your understanding of this person? Then you have reached a milestone in the relationship and there is strong and very convincing reason to continue on to the next gate.

Now that you dropped your jewel into the pond, ask yourself

- *Did my date express openness?*
- *Was I interested and even fascinated?*
- *Did I learn something unexpected?*
- *Do I feel I know this person better?*
- *Am I ready to share something about myself?*

Answers to these questions will help you move the relationship along and on track.

193

☗ *The 4th Gate: Expressing Your Human Vulnerability*

Until now, you have been seeing a person who is capable of accepting and appreciating your gifts of affirmation. You have also given this person the opportunity to share their inner history – the deeper side of their life's story with you. What you heard and felt has enabled you to say that you are ready to continue to the next gate of human vulnerability. Your marriage partner has to be able to show warmth and kindness when you are vulnerable. This next gate will help you understand whether your date has the ability to care for you and be sensitive when you are showing your vulnerability.

The way to prepare your "jewels" for the pond is to understand that as a couple gets to know each other, invariably someone shows a lack of discretion, insensitivity or some minor personal infraction. At the moment it may sting a bit, or is even overlooked. During your initial dates or phone calls there may have been some minor incident which has now been forgotten. Perhaps it was driving too fast for comfort, not giving someone a chance to finish a sentence, permitting your date to spend too much money on a meal that was overpriced and unnecessary, showing up late, not calling when promised., etc. The possibilities are limitless and all a part of being human. Or it can be something more serious, such as a bit of personal information you were holding back until you felt more comfortable.

To pass this gate prepare to apologize for your infraction and select your Inner Circle experience as your emotional anchor. Your apology could sound something like this:

- *"I realized last night that I owe you an apology. When you were expressing your opinion about the role of parents, even though I have other ideas, I cut you off and I shouldn't have."*

- *"I'm sorry I kept you waiting for my call today. I have a tendency to get intensely involved in my meetings and everything else disappears. I'll try to be more considerate."*

- *"Even though we never mentioned it, I'm sure you realize that I struggle with a weight problem. It's something that I'm trying to take seriously and hope to overcome."*

Each of these statements expresses vulnerability. They beg a response and will always elicit one. The response you are looking for will be one of acceptance, understanding and even protectiveness. When it happens a significant moment occurs in the relationship. It has the potential to create a moment of warmth and humanity. Or it can elicit aggressiveness and distancing. If you achieve the right response, it tells you that this is the kind of person you want to spend the rest of your life with. It's important for you to determine that your dating partner has this quality.

⸙ The 5th Gate: Caring

You have traveled through significant milestones in human relationships since beginning your journey through the gates leading to marriage. If your date has passed these initial gates, you should seriously consider moving toward engagement. To do this you have to let your date know that you have the ability to emotionally "encompass" them. Your message has to demonstrate that you have the understanding, sensitivity, determination and commitment to care for this person throughout life. You achieve this by carefully considering your partner's struggles and challenges in life. Then you let this person know that you understand and you care. You don't have answers. Life's challenges don't require answers. They require support and understanding. This is what you are attempting to demonstrate.

Focus on a meaningful memory from your Inner Circle and express yourself with a statement that sounds close to these examples:

- *"I have been thinking about you and your family. It dawned on me that you and your twin brother were quite close. It must have been very difficult for you when he passed away."*

- *"I see that you are a very conscientious person. That's why you work so hard. When I thought about the long hours you put in, the thought of you working under all that pressure really got to me."*

VIII. THE DATING EXPERIENCE

- *I appreciate the time you spend caring for your parents. Their needs and comfort are very important to you. I also understand that it places a great responsibility on your shoulders."*

Each of these statements reflects a respectful, caring and thoughtful involvement in another person's life. When you make them they have an impact. The impact can be seen and heard in the many ripples which form. Your caring statement will give your partner a clear message that their life and struggles are of meaning and importance to you. You need to demonstrate this if you are serious about marriage.

≋ *The 6th Gate: Transformation from "I" to "We"*

You have progressed through five gates of the relationship and you are becoming progressively closer to your goal of marriage. Before you can become engaged you must accept the fact that you have to first disengage. Your disengagement is from your commitments and ties, both conscious and unconscious, to being single. Regardless of how deeply you yearn to marry, you must also accept that you are the lifestyle you lead, even if you live it as an alternative to marriage. You are single in your bank account and IRA, your apartment and furniture, your comings and goings, your name, your friends, eating habits, vacation preferences and so many countless other ways. The next gate will provide you with a perception of being part of a couple.

197

From a dating perspective your goal for this period is to begin seeing yourself as a couple. You achieve this by the following task:

First, focus on your Inner Circle memory. Prepare a place to date where you can have the quiet to take a great risk. Your risk is that you will be planning out the next month or 2 in your relationship with the clear goal of marriage. When the conditions are correct, tell your dating partner:

1. *You have both come a long way with each other and you have been thinking about the possibilities of marriage.*

2. *To see if you are ready to make the commitment for marriage you would like to take a thirty (or more) day period where you will see each or speak to each other on a daily basis.*

3. *You would also like to visit as many of each other's friends and family as possible during this period.*

As you date, you and your partner will slowly develop a greater connection to each other, helping you disengage yourselves from your commitments as singles. The friends and family members you visit will provide you with the support, encouragement and even the "permission" to start thinking of yourselves as a couple. This is how the "I" is transformed into a "We."

VIII. THE DATING EXPERIENCE

☙ *The 7th Gate:*
Engagement and Marriage

Even if you have gotten this far, don't take engagement for granted. And even if you are engaged, don't take the next step lightly. The closer you get, the more carefully you have to tread.

I received a page from Sora, a thirty year old woman, one hour before she was scheduled to meet her dating partner. She knew she was close to being engaged. Her page read: "Shaya, please call Sorah, I have a small question to ask you." I called. Her question wasn't so small. She wanted to know whether I thought she was going too fast and should she delay the engagement. When I questioned her further, she admitted to me that she felt sorry for her older sister who was still unmarried. At first I almost hit the ceiling. Here she was, in her thirties, spending so much of her life trying to become a *Kallah*. She had found the *Chosson* more suited for her than she could have ever hoped for. We knew he would propose that afternoon. Now she was backing out.

The incident reminded my of an absurd parallel from my work many years ago with addicts. I was working with a heroin addict, who happened to be Jewish. In the 60s there were very few Jewish addicts. This one was a true *Nebbich*, a loser. He lived with his mother and rifled through her pocket book daily to grab loose change to buy his drugs. I felt sorry for both of them and invested a great deal of time and effort trying to help him. My efforts began to pay off. He finally agreed to go to a detoxification clinic.

On the day he was supposed to go, he disappeared. Later I tracked him down. He never went. I asked him why he didn't go after he promised me he would. He said that he really intended to. When he was leaving his house in the morning his mother gave him $5.00 for a hair cut. He took the money, bought some heroin and that was it. I then understood very well that his mother's gift was actually an invitation not to leave home. Better stay an addict and stay with me than leave me for a treatment center. That's what happens when individuals are addicted.

I don't mean to equate the two. I do want to say that life styles are impossibly difficult to change. When I hear that Sorah has a small question, or that Channie has already broken 2 engagements, then I understand that it's hard to break a life style. Call it fear, call it anxiety, call it an addiction. It's not a heroin addiction, but it's a real challenge. This step is fraught with countless hazards.

The way to get around these hazards is to make sure you have outside help from someone in the background, a friend, rabbi, rebbetzin or someone else of influence who sees the whole picture and says: "Don't you dare let this opportunity slip away!" Getting engaged is like that youngster jumping off the high board for the first time. It's a change and a step which requires true support and a real push. This is why in every engagement I have coached there has always been two trusted individuals, one for each of the dating partners, who have earned the respect of both and are committed to getting both of them to the *chupah*. The role of your Inner Circle experience is to ground and stabilize you as you get ready for this most important moment in your life. You will need to deal with your anxieties and fears and the pulls that are being exerted by so many forces all around you. Here are some recommendations for planning the moment:

> 1. *Don't let the engagement be a surprise. Plan it out as you are dating, particularly in the transformation stage. Discuss where you will live, employment, friends and every other relevant issue in your future as a couple.*
>
> 2. *Don't think of engagement as breaking out color war or Hollywood fire works. This will only demonstrate that you are both anxious and can't deal with the intimacy and closeness required to move forward from this wonderful moment in your lives.*
>
> 3. *Try to recall your precious moments which have brought you both to the decision to become engaged.*
>
> 4. *Become engaged in a very private way and share it, initially with only those who are most important to both of you.*

IX. The Future of the Inner Circle

☙ The Circle Of Gold

    The future of this program resides in its ability to provide personal and effective guidance to the countless Frum singles in search of their *bashert*. One effective way of providing this service is through the organization The Circle Of Gold- a small group, with shared responsibility among its members.

☙ How the Circle Of Gold Works

    Small groups of 10-15 members experience an Inner Circle workshop together and learn about each other's

IX. THE FUTURE OF THE INNER CIRCLE

needs and dating preferences. The workshop is presented by a The Circle Of Gold leader who is responsible to both lead the workshop and serve as dating coach for all its members. The members of the Circle Of Gold assist one another by providing the leader with suggestions of potential dating partners for each other. These suggestions are appropriately researched and dates are arranged by the leader for Circle Of Gold members. Once a couple is dating, the leader is responsible for coaching each member through the process until engagement and marriage. The group members are also encouraged to maintain ongoing contact with each other, arrange informal gatherings and share in each others triumphs and challenges. Because of the intense nature of the workshop and the profound issues which bind the members, The Circle Of Gold has the potential to serve as a crucial source of support, of belonging and most important, the key of marriage.

In this way a Circle Of Gold's task is to ensure that each of its members has the opportunity to date appropriate people who have been selected by members who recognize each other's needs. The Circle Of Gold's role is not completed until each of its members is married.

≑ *The Global Village*

The Circle Of Gold works within a geographic proximity. We must also address the issue of people spread out through this continent and across the globe. I've heard so many mature singles say that dating is painfully infrequent and there are too few quality people to choose from. One Frum woman told me that she is close to fifty and has not dated more than five times in her entire life. She can meet many potential people to date and one of them may be her *bashert*. However, one may be in NY while your *bashert* is in LA. Your *bashert* may even live around the corner from you. You may even pass each other on the way to the train, but never meet. Now that we know and understand how to make relationships click, bringing two people together is our next critical task.

To achieve this we must learn to take advantage of the revolution in communications- this electronic global village which *Hashem* has brought us to. In this cyber-age of instant global communication, we can help each and every Frum single locate and communicate with that one person, to be your *bashert*. This person may live around the corner or across the continent. In today's world, there really is very little difference. Physical distance can be overcome once we know how to bridge the emotional gap. Our next frontier is harnessing the power of communications toward creating *Shidduchim*. To achieve this, we must also consider electronic Circles Of Gold which bring people together in a shared experience. We can achieve this through learning how to effectively use video Internet conferencing to provide workshops and the same technology to help relationships develop. It's really not so absurd. It may even be safer, and it's certainly faster. Today, the number of Internet websites devoted to *Shidduchim* is proliferating Our program has demonstrated that relationships can reach a stage of readiness for marriage in shorter spans of time because communications are focused on creating meaningful bonds. For example, I am presently working with a couple communicating via e-mail, Fed Exs and faxes and making splendid headway, perhaps even better than they would be able to face to face. The beauty is that when it's done right, the process creates deep and lasting bonds.

These are our next frontiers. It is my wish and *Tefillah* that we can all be witness and participate in the *Simchos* of every *frum* single throughout the world who yearns to find their *bashert* and together build a *Bayis Neeman B'Yisroel*.

X. Work Sheets

☥ Eight Days to Your Inner Circle

Developing each stage of the Inner Circle requires preparation and a deepening of your understanding of each level before you can effectively use these skills on dates. For this reason I have devoted the last section of this book to serve as worksheets which enable you to follow a progressive and well tested course which prepares you for the dating experience. The worksheets and preparations do not include the last two gates of Transformation and Engagement, as these are proactive proposals to initiate new stages in the relationship, rather than being skills oriented.

✤ *Defining Your Inner Circle: 1st Member*

DAY 1.

    A. *Follow the visualization exercises provided in the chapter on the Inner Circle to define the first member of your Inner Circle.*

    B. *After defining your first member hold on to the visual focus of the place and feeling you associate with this member.*

    C. *Take a walk, ride a bike, sit in an easy chair, or do anything else which enables you to hold on to this memory.*

    D. *Phone Focus: Call a friend and strike up a conversation, while holding on to the visual and emotional focus.*

    E. *Observe how your voice, attitude and even friendliness changes while you hold on to this focus.*

    F. *Face to Face: Select a friend, family member or colleague and repeat.*

DAY 2 AND 3:

    Repeat exercise with 2 new members of your Inner Circle.

Day 1

Inner Circle Member _____
_____

Place _____

Feeling_____
_____
_____

Phone Focus _____
_____
_____

To whom _____
_____
_____

Feelings and Observations _____
_____
_____

Face to Face Focus _____

To whom _____
_____
_____

Feelings and Observations

♆ Day 2: Defining Your Inner Circle: 2nd Member

Inner Circle Member _____

_____

Place _____

Feeling_____

_____

_____

Phone Focus _____

_____

_____

To whom _____

_____

_____

Feelings and Observations _____

_____

_____

Face to Face Focus _____

To whom _____

_____

_____

Feelings and Observations

❦ Day 3: Defining Your Inner Circle: 3rd Member

Inner Circle Member _____

Place _____

Feeling _____

_____

_____

_____

Phone Focus _____

_____

_____

To whom _____

_____

_____

_____

Feelings and Observations _____

_____

_____

Face to Face Focus _____

X. Work Sheets

To whom _____

_____

_____

_____

Feelings and Observations _____

_____

_____

_____

_____

_____

_____

_____

_____

_____

_____

_____

_____

DAY 4: Strengthening Your Focus on Hope and Belief

A. As your next step, spend the next day focusing on Hope and Belief. First do the visualizations in the chapter provided on Hope and Belief

B. Hold on to visual focus of hope and belief while you take a walk, ride a bike, sit in an easy chair, or do anything else which enables you to hold this focus.

C. Phone Focus: Call a friend and strike up a conversation, while holding on to the visual and emotional focus.

D. Observe how your voice, attitude and even friendliness changes while you hold on to this focus.

E. Face to Face: Select a friend, family member or colleague and repeat

Describe your focus of Hope _____

_____

_____

_____

_____

_____

_____

_____

X. Work Sheets

_____

_____

Describe your focus of Belief _____

_____

_____

_____

_____

_____

Phone Focus

To whom _____

_____

_____

_____

Feelings and Observations _____

_____

_____

Face to Face Focus _____

To whom _____

Feelings and Observations

⚘ Day 5: Developing Affirmations

A. Choose a friend, family member or colleague at work.
B. Select 3 affirmations related to this person's efforts at helping others, learning Torah or doing other Mitzvos.
C. Write down the affirmations.
D. Select a member of your Inner Circle and imagine saying these affirmations to this person. Anticipate his or her ripples.
E. Phone Focus: Focus on your Inner Circle and call this person. Spend a few moments and then present one of the affirmations. Listen for the ripples and observe the changes in his or her voice and observe the changes in yourself
F. Face to Face: Repeat the Phone Focus procedure as you meet this person Face to Face.

Person to affirm
Describe 3 Affirmations:

1. _____

_____

2. _____

_____

3. _____

_____

Affirmations _____

Phone Focus _____

_____

_____

To whom _____

_____

_____

_____

Feelings and Observations _____

_____

_____

Face to Face Focus _____

To whom _____

_____

_____

_____

Feelings and Observations_____

_____

_____

_____

X. Work Sheets

⚜ Day 6: Developing Inner History Questions

A. Choose a friend, family member or colleague at work.
B. Select 3 Inner History questions related to this person's defining moments in life. For example:
   — How a woman felt the day she brought a new baby home from the hospital.
   — How it felt to meet a Godol or Torah giant in Israel.
   — What did it feel like to approach the Kosel for the first time.
C. Write down the questions.
D. Select a member of your Inner Circle to focus on and imagine asking these questions to this person. Anticipate his or her responses or ripples.
E. Phone Focus: Focus on your Inner Circle and call this person.
   Spend a few moments and then ask the questions. Listen for the ripples and observe the changes in his or her voice and observe the changes in yourself.
F. Face to Face: Repeat the Phone Focus procedure as you meet this person Face to Face.

Person to ask Inner History questions

X. Work Sheets

Describe 3 questions:

1. _____

   _____

2. _____

3. _____

   _____

Inner History

Phone Focus_____

_____

_____

To whom _____

_____

_____

_____

Feelings and Observations _____

_____

_____

Face to Face Focus _____

To whom _____

Feelings and Observations _____

🐚 Day 7: Developing Your Human Vulnerability Skills

A. Choose a friend, family member or colleague at work to whom you can make a minor and even not-so-minor apology.

B. Select an apology which is appropriate to your relationship. For example:
— I owe you an apology for not remembering your birthday
— I'm really sorry I wasn't able to lend you money last week. I was broke.

C. Write down the apology.

D. Select a member of your Inner Circle to focus on and imagine saying this apology to this person. Anticipate his or her responses or ripples.

E. Phone Focus: Focus on your Inner Circle and call this person. Spend a few moments and then say the apology. Listen for the ripples.

F. Observe the changes in voice and friendliness.

G. Observe the changes in yourself.

H. Face to Face: Repeat the Phone Focus procedure as you meet this person Face to Face.

Person to apologize to _____

Describe your Human Vulnerability statement:

1. _____

2. _____

3. _____

Human Vulnerability

Phone Focus _____

_____

To whom _____

_____

_____

Feelings and Observations _____

_____

Face to Face Focus _____

X. Work Sheets

To whom _____

_____

_____

_____

Feelings and Observations _____

_____

_____

_____

_____

_____

_____

_____

_____

_____

_____

_____

_____

_____

_____

≑ Day 8: Developing Your Caring Skills

A. Choose a friend, family member or colleague at work.
B. Select a caring statement related to this person's challenges in life.
   For example:
   — I've been thinking how you burn the candle at both ends to make sure that work doesn't get in the way of your chesed activities.
   — In spite of your reading skills difficulties, I see how you
   really plug away.
C. Write down the Caring statements.
D. Select a member of your Inner Circle to focus on and imagine saying these statements to this person. Anticipate his or her responses or ripples.
E. Phone Focus: Focus on your Inner Circle and call this person. Spend a few moments and then say one statement. Listen for the ripples, observe the changes in his or her voice and observe the changes in yourself.
F. Face to Face: Repeat the Phone Focus procedure as you meet this person Face to Face.

X. Work Sheets

Person to share your caring statements _____

_____

Describe 3 Caring statements:

1. _____

_____

2. _____

_____

3. _____

_____

Caring

Phone Focus _____

_____

_____

To whom _____

_____

_____

_____

Feelings and Observations _____

_____

_____

Face to Face Focus _____

To whom _____

_____

_____

_____

Feelings and Observations _____

_____

_____

X. Work Sheets

XI. EPILOGUE: A Personal Message to Mature Singles

From the very inception of writing this book it has been my desire to create a journey of hope and promise for each of you. I now believe we have gone beyond our lofty dreams and opened a window beyond hope. It is a well defined and traveled pathway which will lead many of you to success in your search for your *bashert*.

XI. Epilogue

As a result of my experiences with so many mature singles who have trusted me and gone through this program, my life has been irrevocably and immeasurably changed. It has resulted in sharing the *Simchos* of older singles who had once believed that "it would take a miracle" to find that one special person.

In reality it did take a miracle. Because marriage is no different than any other life process. All of life is a miracle. Each moment is a miraculous gift from *Hashem*. From a practical perspective, their success was a result of their own efforts. It required focus, determination, inner strength and the courage to stay the course. In the end, they all discovered that they had the ability to recognize their *bashert* when feelings of love, trust and security emerged. They watched as their emotional connections slowly and surprisingly evolved in unexpected ways to create bonds of love and trust. Because at first, there appeared to be no sign that these feelings would ever be felt and shared. In the end we all shared in their joy and *Simcha*. Because of their efforts *Hashgocha* had the opportunity to take hold and fill their lives with happiness. This was the "miracle."

Now I have a new vision. It is to ensure that each and every mature single has access to this approach. Because I and others have been witness to its effectiveness, simplicity and potential for success. It is my fervent hope that that the future will yield other efforts even more effective than mine and I look forward to these developments. Because the task is far too great for my voice or even one hundred like mine. In the end we have no real choice but to devote all our energies to your cause. And we must not to forget even one of you, regardless of your age or experiences. We must remember you not only on *Shabbos* and *Yom Tov*, but every day of the year. And we dare not forget you when we make our own *Simchos*. We must always hear and be sensitive to your yearning and do everything in our power to help you find that one special person with whom you will build your life and family. In the end I believe that arriving at this awareness and commitment alone was enough of a reason for me to embark on this journey.

My wish and *Brocha* is that each of you should build a *Bayis Neemon B'Yisroel* and we shall all be *zoche* to build our families together in *Eretz Yisroel, Bimheira Biyomenu*.